MODELS OF MINISTRY

Afterthoughts on
Fifty Years

MODELS OF MINISTRY

HENRY E. HORN

FORTRESS PRESS
Minneapolis

COPYRIGHT © 1989 BY AUGSBURG FORTRESS

Library of Congress Cataloging-in-Publication Data

Horn, Henry E.
  Models of ministry.

  Bibliography: p.
  1. Pastoral theology.   2. Horn, Henry E.   I. Title.
BV4011.H63   1989   253   88–45241
ISBN 0–8006–2311–8

3452J88   Printed in the United States of America   1–2311

Contents

83281

Acknowledgments

IN PREPARING TO WRITE THIS BOOK, I HAVE used several occasions to thresh out my thoughts: first, addresses to pastors of the Minnesota Synod of the Lutheran Church in America, in January 1985; second, a conference for Minnesota Lutheran campus pastors held in 1985; third, an article in *Circle,* of the National Lutheran Campus Ministry, reporting on the conference; fourth, addresses to the Mountain District of the Pacific Northwest Synod of the Lutheran Church in America, held in Missoula, Montana, in October 1986; fifth, an address to the seniors of the Philadelphia Theological Seminary, in May 1987; and finally, an address to the pastors of the New England Synod of the Lutheran Church in America, in September 1986. I am not unmindful of the grace that listeners bring when they pull imaginative ideas out of an ill-prepared preacher. Thanks!

Introduction

AFTERTHOUGHTS ARE THE SPECIALTY OF many of us. In a way, they are our genre. We may do a good job on a Sunday sermon, but we are also wonderful in adding a Monday review of what we might have said. We prepare a careful manuscript, but the act of speaking before a congregation pulls out marginal dimensions and starts us on Monday reflections concerning what we could have said. People like us should write sermons out on Mondays after we have delivered them.

For me this past year has been a time to recall and celebrate fifty years in the ordained ministry of the church. By sharing my celebration with many of those who have known the ordained ministry intimately, I have been helped toward "Monday afterthoughts." A fund of experience stands there to be surveyed in its totality. From that totality, I seek to speak, hoping that others may not have to develop their understanding of the ordained ministry from scratch but can gain from my experience.

In trying to tie a final knot on the package of this experience, I seek a descriptive text characteristic of my stage of life that will in itself sum everything up. One such text has come to me—all the way through my memory from about the fourth grade and, of course, the King James Version of the Bible:

> Let the people praise thee, O God;
>   let all the people praise thee.
> Then shall the earth yield her increase;
>   and God, even our own God, shall bless us.
> God shall bless us;
>   and all the ends of the earth shall fear him.
> (Ps. 67:5–7)

The meaning in this text has been opened up to me as the result of at least four distinct but intersecting lines of thought. First, it

1

happened that at a time when I was exercising the delicious pre-
rogative of the retired to listen to music through the dozing of an
afternoon nap, a choral group was singing the text of this same
psalm. The note was one of a steady current of praise. But suddenly,
as the choir reached the word "then," the mood changed and the
anthem rushed on in a boisterous torrent of creativity, the thank-
fulness doing its work in the created world, bringing it to full
fruition. I had never before understood the connection between
thanksgiving and the creative work of God so clearly. But now I
looked again at the text and cherished it for the gift that the inter-
preter had given.

Second, this reminded me of some reading I had done years ago
on the Jewish religion, when I was in search of the practice and
meaning of the fundamental building block of Jewish worship, the
berakah or blessing. This blessing is a definite act of body and lip
which accompanies each significant daily action of the worshiper:
arising, dressing, drinking, eating, washing, walking, and the rest.
I remembered a comment by a rabbi about the berakah. He said
we might imagine for the Israeli Jew a large dammed-up lake in
the heights of the Judean mountains. When a worshiper opens up
his life in the gesture and word of thanksgiving to God, the sluice
gate at the bottom of the dam opens automatically and the waters
of God's grace flow out to irrigate the desert of human life, and
the desert is transformed by the bursting of life. It was impossible
not to think of this picture in the light of this interpretation of the
psalm.

Third, for some time I have been worried about a lack of piety
in the Reformation tradition as I see it represented today. In Martin
Luther's rediscovery of the way the gracious God saves us not by
works but by the gracious gift of Jesus Christ that is appropriated
by faith, the emphasis is on the movement of salvation from God
to us—always. The result for many of us is that any remaining
trace of a discipline of works has come to be frowned on. Thus,
our tradition has edged toward emphasizing the gift of God exclu-
sively. And we have come to receive that gift in constant penitence:
penitence has become the characteristic and visible sign of our piety.
In a recent study, the Reformed theologian Brian Gerrish turns to
the other side of Luther, where he finds that the flavor of the life
of the forgiven is constant thanksgiving.[1] What is more, Gerrish
finds that in this, Luther and Calvin are at one. In fact, the first

question of the Heidelberg Catechism asks what the main aim of the religious life is, and it answers, It is to praise God and worship him forever. Gerrish consequently asks why Lutherans and those in the Reformed tradition do not get on with it and develop some disciplines of thanksgiving. What he seeks is a movement beyond the "then" of the psalm. Of course, there have been some significant attempts in Protestant history to move in this direction. Yet in almost every case, what has evolved is a definite set of things to do and attitudes to cultivate—a set of prescriptions enthroned as fundamentally necessary. That, however, looks like "works," and therefore those in our tradition back away. But is there not room for developing our own disciplines in some sort of evangelical freedom? The shapes of our disciplines need not be the same, but there should be some responsive disciplines of thanksgiving to sustain the life of praise. We must develop disciplines within a structure that both makes sense to the believer and shows forth the goodness of God to others.

Fourth, all of this coincides with my mood after fifty years of ordained ministry. It is not simply that I carry with me rich memories that I recognize as the gift of God. Forty years ago, after about ten years as a minister, I faced the prospect of a well of ideas run dry. As a precaution, I decided to capture on paper those moments when I was surprised—wherever and whenever. The discipline of writing notes of surprise and thanksgiving took some years to develop. (I shall say more in chapter 3.) Now, as I survey fifty years of ministry, I have ninety-eight volumes of notes, ninety-eight volumes capturing events of thanksgiving, of "thens." For me, *this is it: thanksgiving and in my very own experience!* I can thus vibrate to a piece of music that translates all these events of memory into one text!

But then, I thought, if I am going to use this text for any purpose in the church, I should strengthen my case by consulting other scriptural versions and the commentaries. So I looked at the other versions. And you can guess what happened, because it has happened to you. There is no "then" in any of them! In fact most of them deemphasize the thanksgiving. The composer is left with an old version! In this day of historical-critical methods, that has happened to many a good text and sermon of mine. Often the discovery has been made after the fact—in Monday afterthoughts!

Now, however, after a long ministry I do not take such disappointments lying down. Was it not Luther who, from his own
experience, found the text that had revealed the truth to him so
compelling that he wrote the word "only" in the margin? In this
case, I have the testimony of the composer of music, the suggestion
of the effect of thanksgiving from the Jewish tradition, the urging
of Luther and Calvin for us to get on to the life of thanksgiving,
and the ninety-eight volumes of testimony from my own experience. Is this not enough to underline the "then" again?

In biblical studies today, we are finding voices that urge us to
go beyond the text.[2] Up to this time, our biblical studies have tried
to bring us the exact text or as close as we can come to the text.
That is the final aim, though in the process we wander into imaginative thinking—all of which seems to end with an accepted
text. In the use of Scripture in preaching and the devotional life,
should we not engage the text through imaginative thinking? Is
there not a halo beyond the text? Should we not move from the
indicative to the subjunctive—from what is to what could be?

As I have grown older, I have been fascinated by the last words
of the *Didache* (ca. A.D. 230), *The Teaching of the Twelve Disciples:*
"And allow the prophets to give thanks as much as they wish . . ."
Very evidently the vision of those who in thanks move from the
indicative to the subjunctive mood are necessary for the community
of faith. It is with confidence in that, that I offer these thoughts.

> Let the people praise thee, O God;
>   let all the people praise thee.
> Then shall the earth yield her increase;
>   and God, even our own God, shall bless us.
> God shall bless us;
>   and all the ends of the earth shall fear him.

The chapters that follow will organize my thanksgiving of today.
They deal with shapes, models of ordained ministry. The doctrine
of the ministry is a controversial one in our churches at present.
Most of the effort is directed at unearthing shapes and models of
centuries ago. There is very little discussion of the ways in which
human lived experience can itself evolve. I hope these discussions
will help.

Several years of postretirement teaching in seminaries have
brought me, at the end of my ministry, close to those who are
about to put on models of ministry as a uniform. There are the

attendant fears that they cannot fit their own integrity into old models. Many students would like to allow their own integrity, as they have experienced it, to shape what they do. Though congregations desire integrity in the ministry, they at bottom move in model expectations; and this makes the first call for these seminarians fraught with struggle. On the other hand, one who has celebrated fifty years in the ministry knows that one passes, usually in ten years, from a situation in which the model shapes the person to that where experience shapes the model. I speak to the model from experience.

Furthermore, wondrous things have happened around us in these fifty years, most of which are gathered up in human studies today. I have had the advantage of living in the watchtower of the university, where these movements have taken place, and they have affected my own understanding of our ministry. I have chosen five areas where models of ministry have developed through an interchange of faithful ministry and human developments: the areas of scriptural interpretation, faith development, the discerning of spirits, ritual leadership, and leadership in the civic space. The areas translate into five models of the ordained minister as preacher and teacher, pastor, prophet, priest, and citizen.

I will make abundant use of the first person in the following chapters because it is my intention to interweave my own experience with the human developments in my accounts. That is how things have intertwined in the living of a long ministry of twenty-five years in the university world. Though it is natural for a campus minister to talk from the university viewpoint, it is certainly my assumption that what I say is relevant to the ministry as a whole and to members of congregations everywhere.

> Let the people praise thee, O God;
>   let all the people praise thee.
> Then shall the earth yield her increase;
>   and God, even our own God, shall bless us.
> God shall bless us;
>   and all the ends of the earth shall fear him.

MODEL ONE	*Scriptural Interpretation*

AT HOME IN MY STUDY THERE IS A FILING cabinet with two large drawers filled to the brim with sermon outlines. If I open these drawers the sermons spill out. Right there is a good part of my ministerial life, and the urge often rises to dig through this mine for nuggets of lasting value. The life, however, has gone out of the words. All that is left are written words pointing to something. When I first preached them, I could feel a strange liveliness somewhere in the field between my mouth and the people's ears. In fact, this electric atmosphere brought forth much more than was in the writing. That was proved to me on the occasion of the fiftieth-anniversary celebration of my ordination. I have several volumes of letters of appreciation, each letter citing some situation or event surrounding preaching which I remember vividly.

Long ago in seminary, I was taught to take the biblical text seriously, to use all my human gifts and training to unlock its meaning. That was to be done by knowing the author and his or her intentions, the situation that provoked the text, the place of the text in the surrounding material, what literary genre it was and how it should be interpreted, and what oral background in real life might have prompted it. In trying to be faithful to this way of proceeding, I have grasped whatever help I could get from the scholarly work around me, on the one hand, and from wide reading, on the other. I was always gratefully surprised when these two tracks came together in a fundamental insight.

PERSONAL BACKGROUND

My own background in biblical knowledge was not unlike that of most of us in American Protestantism. I was nourished at home by storytelling. My parents believed that children should hear stories so that they could become familiar with biblical figures and allusions. This cultural necessity was reinforced throughout my schooling by memorable teachers who assumed that biblical knowledge was part of the cultural atmosphere in which we lived. I was always grateful to my parents when, even in college, I would answer the queries of my professors on biblical allusions of which, strangely to me, others seemed ignorant.

It was the Bible picture book of Gustave Doré that supplied my childhood imagination. Etched in my brain somewhere, and constantly recalled, are the especially lugubrious sections of Scripture that children remember best: the creation of Adam and Eve; the dismissal from the Garden of Eden; Abraham's attempt to sacrifice Isaac; the flood; the tower of Babel; Moses giving the Ten Commandments; Joshua commanding the sun to stand still; Daniel in the lion's den; Shadrach, Meshach, and Abednego in the fiery furnace. I know that the lurid lines of these romantic pictures had their effect on me. Strangely, what I now regard as the gracious and most compelling parts of Scripture—the prophets, Jesus' ministry of healing and teaching, and the New Testament letters—made little impression then. A more modern picture book in full color replaced the Doré for my younger siblings, and its pictures were not as compelling.

In all of this, each story stood by itself; there was never any connecting thread tying the stories together. And in my memory, which always tends to remember in distinct frames, the single acts of memory kept everything in a sort of card catalogue of biblical material.

In those days, the Sunday-school movement was in full force.[1] Each church had its Sunday-school, and attendance there frequently exceeded that at the church worship. Certainly the Sunday schools were often only very loosely connected with the churches themselves, as neophyte pastors were amazed to find out. The Sunday-school movement began in the English-speaking world as an interdenominational lay development. Now in retrospect we are beginning to recognize that it really came out of English evangelicalism with a strong Methodist flavor. This flavor extended to its theology as well as its worship. The evangelical revival experience was central to its life; and the gospel song was its weekly confession.

In each Methodist congregation there were a number of "band leaders" whose duty it was to supervise groups of members, or "bands." The leaders watched over the members' lives and promoted the disciplines of Christian piety. The Sunday-school movement inherited this tradition with its Sunday-school teachers—laypersons without appreciable training in biblical interpretation. Most in my day carried with them their chief tool of interpretation: the Scofield Bible.[2] In the Sunday school, biblical material was conveyed largely in single-frame stories. Any thread holding one story to another was supplied by Scofield's notes. Little did I know then that Scofield's thread carried the invariable presupposition of the inerrancy of the text. It was only in my mature years that I realized how sectarian this simple Bible tool was and yet how it influenced the biblical view of thousands of persons.

For us, then, the Bible was a book set apart, a holy book—unlike other literature, an inerrant book. Our primary aim seemed to be to defend the book's inerrancy. Sometimes we took a passage in a crudely literal way; other times we went on a roundabout journey to escape literal interpretation, bringing some deus ex machina to the rescue of inerrancy. Every attempt at scholarly investigation was met by defensive maneuvers.

All of that was part of our Sunday-school training. Yet we were also growing up in the church. After our evangelical experience in the Sunday school and our gospel songs, we would go upstairs to worship. We expected the pastor to preach from his knowledge of the scriptural text. We assumed that he got his knowledge by virtue of the tools and the reading to which he had been introduced in the special education of the seminary. There was no hint that the two ways of interpreting Scripture—the Sunday-school way and the seminary way—were at odds with each other. Sunday-school teachers, in my experience, were always cooperative with their minister. They were loved by their students, did a tolerably good job of caring for them, and often became exemplary models of Christian living.

SPACE FOR OSCILLATION

The problem arising from the gap between the methods and knowledge of the Sunday school and the professional experience of the minister was left to the minister to work with in a pastoral way. The poles of Sunday school and seminary marked the space within which the minister lived and worked; in fact he carried them with him constantly. Every minister then was both his frontier and his home base in one space.

Aren't we all? D. W. Winnicott has portrayed the activity of a toddler with her mother in the park as modeling the shape of our whole life.[3] The mother takes the child into the middle of the park, and then lets the child explore. The toddler scoots away, tasting freedom to the limit. At the limit, anxiety springs up and overwhelms her. She turns around to see if her mother is still in sight, and then she runs back and clings to her home base. Again and again she does this, trying out an ever farther frontier and therewith increasing the anxiety of her mother, but always running back home. Winnicott tells us that this sort of behavior is typical of our life's path. Even when our children leave home for college, we know that we should keep their rooms for them, because the other side of their growing life is coming home. Thus there is always a growing edge or frontier where one tries out one's independence and a home base to which one returns. Life oscillates between the two. Really to know another person, we must know both the person's frontier and the person's home base.

Certainly I shall never outgrow the clear, distinct lines of my own home base. There is a fundamental necessity for home to be solid and unchangeable. For growth, however, it is necessary to move constantly to new frontiers. Our character takes shape as we try to handle the oscillation between the two poles.

One of my seminary professors held that the majority of his students came with a firm base of knowledge received in childhood and shaped by confirmation instruction. In three years of seminary their frontiers were stretched, he assumed. When the seminary years were over, however, the students returned to the theology of their earlier training. Their confirmation instruction became the theology they taught in their ministry. Hearing that, I determined then and there that it should not be so in my ministry. I thus started out on a long journey. My ministerial life coincides almost exactly with the various developments in scriptural interpretation that have brought Continental methods of scholarship to the American ministry. During these fifty years, I have seen the steady climb of Old and New Testament scholarship in the seminary and finally in ecumenical discussion. That journey is a tale to be told. Better to have a pilgrim on this road tell the tale.

SEMINARY DAYS

In the 1930s, Old Testament studies had not roused themselves at all. In fact, I could not think of a duller subject than seminary work in the Old Testament. True, some decades before, new theories had been proposed. There was the scholarship of Julius Wellhausen, who examined the texts of the first five books of the Old Testament and suggested that different narrative accounts lay on the surface side by side. These he labeled J, for the word Yahweh, used for God; E, for the word Elohim, used for God; D, for a style such as we have in Deuteronomy from later writers of the prophets' time; and P, for a priestly rewriting in exilic times. Other studies showed the Book of Isaiah to be in three parts, each of which seemed to have been from a different time. And books such as Daniel were assigned a radically new date that upset all of the Scofield calculations about the future.

But this was irrelevant for us, because in our lessons for the regular liturgy in those days we never used the Old Testament. If we were not going to use the texts, what was the use of digging into their meaning? My professor of Old Testament nevertheless spent most of his time denouncing Wellhausen and his theories, theories that his students had only faintly discerned. At a fellowship banquet, a few of us made up some ditties spoofing the professors, and we offered them in quartet form to Gospel tunes. I remember our quip on the Old Testament professor:

> _____ walks with me and he talks with me,
> And he tells me I must *beware*
> Of J, D, and E, redacted by P;
> Wellhausen is only a snare.

It was one of those incidents where young people giggle alone. No one else was amused! The subject was still too hot to handle.

It was not till about the end of World War II that new interest in the Hebraic world developed in America. Then creativity in Old Testament studies burgeoned. We began to see that a good deal of the Reformation could be understood as Luther rediscovering the Hebraic dimensions of Christianity and bringing these through the Greek tradition to the present. So all-compelling was this revolution that we used to say in the 1960s, "Go through your library and throw out all Old Testament studies before about the year 1945. It is now a new era." I shall speak of this later when I describe biblical theology in the fifties.

New Testament studies had moved beyond listlessness by the time I was in the seminary. In Europe, the use of historical criticism to decide questions of authorship, situation, and the source materials *behind* the text had been accepted for some fifty years—at least in the universities, though the churches lagged behind. In American Protestantism in the thirties, however, one had to be brave to speak out. Our New Testament professor was a warm, devout German who spoke a soft, stuttering English that few understood easily. If one listened closely, however, one could learn of the latest scholarly findings.[4] The few students who did listen caught the enthusiasm. I remember one of the best, who was so freed of his bondage to the doctrine of inerrancy that he rejoiced in his discovery before the committee examining him for ordination. That ended his hope of joining the ministry in our communion. I often wonder what happened to him. He would have been a wonderful teacher.

A course in English Bible was really what opened to us the advances in historical-critical studies. This course was offered by the professor of Christian education,[5] and it aimed at exposing ministers-to-be to those sections of Scripture which were largely ignored in our Sunday-school training: the prophets, Jesus of the Gospels, the letters of the New Testament.

When our professor reached the threefold structure of Isaiah, several students, shocked within their inerrancy cocoons, made a stir. The investigating committee that was brought in was disconcerted by what was happening in the scholarly field and would not pursue the matter. The whole experience, however, left the professor apprehensive. The course—possibly the most exciting in the seminary and certainly the most popular—was dropped. The time was not right.

LEADING THE CHURCH
TO A STATEMENT

Meanwhile nationally there was a controversy in the churches over the interpretation of Scripture. Of course one would find the side of inerrancy defending our common home base: that is part of us. The question was who would come out to defend what was happening on the frontier. At that time, historical-critical studies were in a generally negative phase; they had not yet attained many of the positive effects they would eventually have on those who sought in them a springboard to preaching.

For our church two of my seminary professors took the lead. The first was my New Testament professor, whose German training and warm, devout manner made him generally beloved and never resented as a competitor. The other was the professor of church history, who in training at Leipzig had inhaled the new methods.[6] Both had experience with the German professors and pastors who had led the previous generation from the doctrine of inerrancy to a tentative acceptance of the new methods of historical criticism without bringing damage to fundamental faith. Both were absent a great deal from the seminary and on their return gave reports of what was happening in national discussions among Lutherans.

The document that resulted from the discussions was important to me because, I see in retrospect, it freed my ministry from the start to embrace the frontiers in scholarly research, it launched me on the currents and waves, and it has beached me on the shores of imagination today.[7] The position the document defended is this:

1. The Scriptures are the "only rule and standard according to which all dogmas and teachers are to be esteemed and judged."
2. The Word of God is used in different senses in Scripture.
3. The basic Word is the gospel, that is, the "message concerning Jesus Christ, His life, His work, His teaching, His suffering and death, His resurrection and ascension for our sakes, and the saving love of God made manifest in Him."
4. This Word of God is in the life of his people through all ages.
5. The Word of God is preserved in the Scriptures. They are the channel of God's Word and therefore can be called the Word.
6. All books of the Bible are judged in relation to the gospel.
7. Holding these truths to be true, we believe that the Scriptures are
   (*a*) the spring from which the saving power of God continuously flows into the lives of persons;
   (*b*) the only source of truly Christian doctrine; and
   (*c*) the only rule and norm for Christian faith and life.

Running through this text is the influence of the Luther studies then current. Luther had exhibited a strange polarity in his interpretation of Scripture. On the one hand, he had shown a dogged literalism almost to the point of assuming inerrancy in his use of proof texts; on the other, he had felt that there was a canon within the New Testament canon—that is, that the Scriptures were to be judged individually as they showed forth Jesus Christ as our Lord. On that basis he had dared to rank the books in order of importance. Moreover, he had even dared to insert the word "only" in places where imagination compelled one to underline the text. This has always produced for the Lutheran tradition a sort of aura around the text— a space for prophetic movement where the imagination can work and receive a message from the God who can do the new thing.

The document had the effect, not fully understood at the time, of lifting a weight from the historical-critical study of Scripture in the seminaries and of allowing us to deal with the Bible as we would with any human literature, bringing in the full human dimensions of oral and written materials. It became a sort of Magna Charta for our church concerning scriptural interpretation. Some of us simply will not allow that work to be undone, for we have gained a whole ministry of excitement in interpreting to our people.

As I remember, the document had to be carefully guided through the convention. Most of the delegates carried the home position of inerrancy as a banner. Because, however, they were respectful of their professors and appreciated the devotion and pastoral care in the statement, they were willing to compromise. It has taken us a half century to enter into the inner struggles that this statement launched. Only in the past few years has there been a churchwide program to train laity in what has been accomplished.

FIRST STEPS IN MINISTRY

I started my ministry in a parish where the gap between Sunday-school instruction and what was preached at the church's worship service was huge.[8] We had one of those very large Sunday schools, independently organized, with some forty classes and class leaders. The classes were allowed to determine their own agendas. Some teachers used materials prepared by the denomination—an international series with a denominational slant. Others taught directly from the Bible—usually a Scofield Bible. I can still bring to mind the memory frames of individual teachers—probably clearer models of Christian living than I was as a pastor. They were individually respectful of the pastor and usually very attentive to what I said.

The burden of the gap that I knew to exist between my own method and conclusions and theirs was mine alone. There was no one to talk to about this. We had not yet devised pastoral study groups around the lessons. Added to my confusion was my inexperience in using higher criticism and historical-critical methods to pick at the meaning of the text. The whole complex discipline of exegesis—of finding out what the meaning of the text was to the original audience—was something that later evolved and today is a necessity for the preacher. Then, it had not entered my consciousness. Textual criticism in those days seemed largely negative to those whose home base was inerrancy. It had to be negative in order to clear the ground for positive building on new foundations.

How often I would preach on a shabby text, only to find out later that what I had said fell apart in my own mind on Monday! It was a painful period for me. Fortunately the congregation chose what to believe and brought me through.

COMING OUT INTO THE CLEAR

I was brought out of this first period by an older pastor, a pioneer in biblical studies. He invited me to lead a conference of pastors in a discussion of form criticism. That led me into a frantic search for all I could learn about this new discipline. Form criticism was a search within the text for forms of narratives, poems, bodies of teaching, and understandings of life situations which would illumine the text. Since most of the New Testament grew out of the church's preaching, this was an attempt to penetrate to stages in the tradition earlier than the written word, where an oral tradition of proclamation rather than actual writing contained the message.

One encountered stories, sayings, creeds, fables, legends, myths, parables, miracle stories, pronouncement stories, proverbs. By looking through the text to see the form at an earlier level one penetrated to the oral period where human imagination and enthusiasm colored the material. This brought me into the friendly world of preaching, the world I faced in the pulpit. All of a sudden, the Scriptures were revealing material for preaching. A new era had arrived for me, an era of lively preaching.

Soon thereafter, I left the parish ministry to care for a small college, where I also taught a course in English Bible.[9] The course looked at the Bible as literature. It was a required course, and ecumenical charity was necessary in order to accommodate young women from a wide variety of denominations. The course reflected the popular movement in American colleges of treating the Bible as part of our culture, and it sought to enlarge the students' general cultural understanding.

I organized the course to be very much like my seminary course in English Bible. We started with the prophets, mainly because with them the first historical materials were gathered—but also because the students knew nothing about them. The prophets were new and engaging to the students, though the examination papers I received were hardly flattering to my teaching. There was a quiz on the prophet Amos—a five-minute quiz at the start of class—for which I received a truly memorable answer: "Amos was a humble pheasant," the student wrote. "He received a call from God to go out and phrophesy." The content of his "phrophecy" the student presented well, and then she continued, "But no one would listen, and so Amos gave up phrophesying and went back to being the humble pheasant."

The course was a success if the aim was to acquaint students with the Bible as cultural lore. One could teach that without facing directly the problems of inspiration. Moreover, while reading the Bible as literature, one had the feeling that further studies of the various types of literature involved would yield new horizons for biblical study.

MY SECOND NAIVETÉ

The next period in my biblical journey came in the early fifties when I first arrived in Cambridge. Biblical theology was just beginning to get a foothold. Little paperback volumes in the series on biblical theology carried me deep into biblical concepts and enlivened my preaching on texts. Biblical theology was founded on distinctive "acts of God" that separated certain monumental events like the exodus and the giving of the Ten Commandments from other history. The sequence of these revelatory events made up biblical history quite apart from what was happening elsewhere. In line with this distinctive way of thinking, Israel's history was seen as a story of salvation. Theological concepts were developed from within this channel of biblical life, and it was assumed that there was a natural unity in the biblical material. In biblical history we were introduced to the language of the Bible, the world of Israel, and the whole Hebraic background as contrasted with the world outside.

For me, this development coincided with a new understanding of the Jewish background of Christianity. I read deeply in Jewish writing, particularly in the works of Martin Buber. This prepared me for what the biblical-theology advocates were saying. For instance, in pondering the difference between the thinking of the Bible and secular thinking today, I came across this quotation from Martin Buber's *Moses,* which has stayed in the front of my mind ever since:

> The concept of miracle which is permissible from the historical approach can be defined at its starting point as an abiding astonishment. The philosophizing and the religious person both wonder at the phenomenon, but the one neutralizes his wonder in ideal knowledge, while the other abides in that wonder; no knowledge, no cognition, can weaken his astonishment. Any casual explanation only deepens the wonder for him. The great turning-points in religious history are based on the fact that again and ever again an individual and a group attached to him wonder and keep on wondering; at a natural phenomenon, at a historical event, or at both together; always at something which intervenes fatefully in the life of this individual and this group. They sense and experience it as a wonder . . . but an incident, an event which can be fully included in the objective, scientific nexus of nature and history; the vital meaning of which, however, for the person to whom it occurs, destroys the security of the whole nexus of knowledge for him, and explodes the fixity of the fields of experience named "Nature" and "History." Miracle is simply what happens; in so far as it meets people who are capable of receiving it, or prepared to receive it, as miracle . . . the normal and ordinary can also undergo a transfiguration into miracle in the light of the suitable hour.[10]

This Buberian duality between miracle and history, between wonder and routine acceptance, I quickly adopted as my own, and I gobbled up each volume of biblical theology as it came out. My preaching soon became my kerygma. Other compelling themes came into my thinking: *diakonia, koinonia, marturia.*

Krister Stendahl used to talk of the Christian as a "bilingual" person.[11] His experience as a multilingual person had let him know how in ordinary speech a word from another language can suddenly enrich the whole conversation, causing one to feel an "Aha!" or a "Eureka!" My own thinking has been enriched by Edward Schillebeeckx's use of discoveries from scientific investigation as part of a dual-tracked approach to spirituality, an approach incorporating the way of human studies and the way of traditional piety. Usually one keeps human studies and traditional piety in separate channels. But in the many places where the two tracks cross, the one track often illumines the other through a "searchlight effect."

By the fifties, my new tasks in the university world made me read extensively in every available field, in order to talk intelligently with students and faculty. At the same time I was reading hungrily in the new biblical-theology writers. I hope that in my preaching, the two tracks occasionally came together to spark an "Aha!" Fresh in my memory are two diametrical comments on my preaching. One was made by a medical doctor who wondered when I would come out of biblical language and talk in the twentieth century. The other was made by a professor of theology who took me to task for preaching "anthropology" (human studies) and wondered when I would proclaim the kerygma (the apostolic gospel). Despite my evident confusion, there was no lack of material from which to preach; and it opened readily to life as it opened to me in human studies. That became my style. I had arrived at a new plateau.

Paul Ricoeur employs the term "second naiveté" to refer to that high ground one can come to after experiencing the collapse of one's first naiveté of home and after coming through the wilderness where the "masters of suspicion" hold sway. In the second naiveté one arrives at a quite different prospect.[12] For me this was it! I found in the Hebraic thought of the Old Testament a whole gamut of pictures in words—a walkway to the poetic. I saw that in the original languages the Scriptures were anything but one-dimensionally literal accounts. This discovery freed me to preach.

LITERARY FORMS

We are treated to further excitements of the imagination in the discoveries of scholars like Amos Wilder who worked at mapping the literary genres of Scripture. Starting with Wilder's book *Early Christian Rhetoric*[13] and continuing in his recent book *Jesus' Parables and the War of Myths*,[14] there has been an effort to expose a variety of literary shapes so as to open up the human imagination in interpretation:

The motive for this inclusive approach to the development of method has been Wilder's conviction that in interpretation one must be as responsive as possible to all aspects of knowing and consciousness, and thus to all modalities of man's world belonging, including his rootedness in empirical life and relationships. Hence, Wilder's motive has been to understand the language in all of its dimensions—personal, historical, and social—or, in other words, to understand the operations of the imagination and the heart.[15]

The exposure of the multiform literary genres in Scripture has generated the storytelling rage that is sweeping through theological education today. The story—the narrative form—is now considered the best literary medium to carry a person across the routines of life to the borders of human knowledge and experience which are the frontiers of transcendence. One uses stories such as the narrative of Christmas to show meaning. The Christmas tale starts with Mary and Joseph, who have concerns about the necessities of everyday life. They start a journey that is necessary but upon which Jesus' birth takes place in a strange way. The story then moves to the thresholds of life, between earth and heaven, and even stranger things happen in a new language, accompanied by fear and anxiety. Finally we are left with the doors of heaven ajar and the sound of those around the heavenly throne doing their eternal thing: singing. Such are the possibilities of stories, and the stories of Scripture are perfectly set to open up our imaginations to the questions, What if this is so? What then can be?

Students are trained to tell their own stories and to enflesh their comments on Scripture as story too. Unfortunately, a lot of second-rate stories of human experience that are not worth the telling have been pushed on congregations. We should search for stories that can move to the limits of life, the thresholds of new dimensions, and there imagine in pictures. The Bible is full of stories of this kind. Almost every text hides such a story. In the telling of stories, then, why not a revival of the stories held in the words and word pictures of Scripture?

ENTER THE IMAGINATION

This leads us to the final plateau I have reached in biblical interpretation. Most of my struggles have been to free my own imagination through the text: to seek in the text itself the imagination that brought it to be and then to take a further step, that of engaging the imagination to move from the text as it has now become to what it encourages us to be. If we use the imagination in discerning the journey—the living pilgrimage—of the text to what it now is, shall we not also use the imagination in encouraging its journey through the people of God? If we find the living Word beneath the text, should we not release its living force in the lives of the church? Here the words of Walter Brueggemann in describing the work of Bernhard Anderson are helpful:

> The interface of the claim of the text and the methods of interpretation required concerns the watershed of canon. The moment of canonization divides the dynamics of *how the text came to be* from the dynamics of *how the text causes to be*. It is hardly disputed that in the text *coming to be,* the factors of liberated social possibility, anticipatory psychology, literary finesse and theological accountability have been operative. All of that is present in the formation of the text, and our methods reflect that. The kind of interpretation for which Anderson calls, I suggest, is a recognition that these same factors are operative in the text *causing to be* in the communities that claim these texts as normative and canonical. In that way, the imaginative power that *formed the text* may be continued to be *received from the text*. But such a receiving from the text requires a mode different from the flat literalism of obscuranticism or the flat historicism of rational positivism. The key to a legitimate receiving from the text is to recognize that the text belongs to its lord, or as Anderson says, "God speaks to his people today through the Scriptures at the point of our imagination, that is, where the 'inspired writing' meets the 'inspired reader' and becomes the word of God." Or perhaps as Ricoeur says, the Poem belongs to the Poet, seen and heard, so the text continues to be a medium of *disclosure* that no method of interpretation is free to *close*.[16]

A GENERATION'S VOICE OF THANKSGIVING

This is where the current of biblical scholarship has borne this preacher in half a century. I have come a long way, and the church has too. For a good portion of the journey, I have had to carry the gap between new interpretation and old understanding in silence, for fear of doing injury to fellow Christians. Basically, I carried their battle within me too. There has been that oscillation from frontier to home base, certainly, until I came out in my second naiveté. Both poles have been part of me. Perhaps my generation has been too silent! Would not all of us have made greater progress if we had broken our silence and testified to our thanksgiving for the journey with all its hardships? We have been through the masters of suspicion and have come out at a second naiveté. We can testify that it is not true that if one begins to poke around in the structures of Scriptures, the whole house will fall down. Instead, if one can persevere in the journey, the whole discipline of preaching becomes a great experience, the Scriptures open up their meaning, and the imaginations of hearers are engaged.

There are exciting things happening around us, though. In my church, a churchwide emphasis on Word and witness has opened up the content of Scripture as interpreted by scholarly methods to the rank and file of the congregations. One has to treat such training, however, with integrity: one has to agree to give time and energy over a long time to take the study seriously, meanwhile talking about it with others. It is no longer true that only a few clergy are on this frontier.

Second, there is now an ecumenical consensus concerning scriptural interpretation. This is the product of biblical studies in the last twenty-five years—much of it from the day of biblical theology. Denominational coloring to scholarship is largely a thing of the past. Roman Catholics, Episcopalians, Presbyterians, members of the United Church of Christ, Methodists, Baptists, and Lutherans share in providing scholarly helps for the interpretation of each Sunday's lessons. This ecumenical sharing is a massive step toward the future of our life together and toward the reestablishment of the integrity of the pulpit.

Third, within our liturgies there is an enlarged exposure to the possibility of biblical preaching. Two traditions stretch behind us. First, there is that of Catholic Christendom, where standard lessons have traditionally been used for centuries—the same each year— thus providing a frame-by-frame exposure of Scripture to worshipers. (Even this excluded the Old Testament till about thirty years ago.) Second, there is the tradition of reading Scripture publicly in continuous fashion, generally book by book. This is a Protestant change meant to spur us to take seriously biblical interpretation in worship.

With the renewal of worship in all the churches, the general acceptance of three-year lessons ecumenically, and within this scheme, the setting-aside of certain seasons for the continuous study of individual books, the opportunities for a fresh start are favorable.

These changes coincide with the influence today of redaction criticism—that is, the separate study of the characteristics of individual
writers. The results are eagerly devoured by young preachers who
gather in groups to study the lessons ahead of time. This sets the
stage for a possible reactivation of biblical preaching—and brings
forth my personal thanksgiving!

MODEL	*Faith*
TWO	*Development*

IN OUR DISCUSSION OF THE FIRST MODEL OF ministry—that concerning scriptural interpretation—we unearthed a developmental process of different stages. In our study of faith development we shall detect intertwinings with the first model.

In 1982, the Lutherans in this country celebrated the seventy-fifth anniversary of the first religious work directed specifically toward college students in universities. By chance, this time span coincides almost exactly with the rise of studies of adolescence in psychology: the coining of the word "adolescence" occurred just over seventy-five years ago. Thus, the work of my father and me in the campus ministry from 1917 till 1978[1]—with some gaps—is concurrent with developments in the psychology of adolescence. Moreover, it has been in the past thirty years that human studies in the university have burgeoned, carrying us to the present. The story that unfolds is one of understanding how young human beings grow out of childhood and through the changes of adolescence to where they dare to act, in trust, on their own.

TWO GENERATIONS AGO

My father sensitized the church of the first decades of this century to the needs of college students. Faced with a whole new generation of students—the first generation of his denomination to enter the universities—he was not willing for them to take a vacation from the nourishment of Christian growth in worship, scriptural study, and prayer. He was, furthermore, fearful that the church might lose its promising leaders.[2] Throughout the land it was characteristic of congregations to concentrate power in the hands of the old and to deny it to the young. To him, there was *no* assurance that, without the regular discipline of churchgoing, young people would maintain any connection with the church.

23

For him, an answer was for the church to move into the university community, doing its "own thing," namely, celebrating Word and Sacrament in a gathering of worshipers. He thought that there should be an open-ended organization—at that time called an association—where the university's young between the ages of about seventeen and twenty-five could serve as leaders. This would allow them to grow into informed and experienced leaders for their later church life. Their church education would happen from within the fellowship and thus become an unconscious and subconscious reality.

To carry out his ideas, he left an important New York City congregation and moved to Cornell at a sizable decrease in salary. He organized the Lutheran Association of Ithaca on the principles he had embraced, with marvelous result.[3] Students returning to college after World War I responded quickly to this. They were *eager* to enter into the leadership of the church. The association grew by leaps and bounds. A church building was erected. As soon as this happened the association moved into the building and adopted so many of the habits and manners of churchgoing that much of the pristine life of the association disappeared into respectability. But in those early days of excitement a satellite association was formed in Greater Boston—later to become University Lutheran Church, where I served for twenty-five years.

My father's Protestant colleagues in the campus ministry had another philosophy. They assumed that when students entered college, they made a real break with the community of the church and home. *That* belonged to their childhood. They now entered a sort of interim world—between childhood and adulthood—where they should be free of any entangling connections with the past, in order to test out their own ideas and ideals. If the church was to reach out to them, it would have to do so by methods and in content belonging to the world of the university and the future. These ministers assumed that when college was over the necessities of adult life would bring students to take up again the threads of their former life at home; they would "settle down" and, then, when the family came, would return to the church as members. Such campus ministers could, therefore, be complacent in their attitude and not worry excessively about the students in college. Like the changing of the seasons, the time of return would come. The campus minister's job was to adapt to the university world and challenge the thinking and routines of university-age students.

INITIAL PROBINGS

It was in my father's campus ministry that I grew up. I was thoroughly immersed in the worship and life of the church while at college, and I served as president of the church council. This experience established my choice of vocation. I decided to enter the ministry with the campus as my field of specialization. But it was not till I was forty that I received a campus call. I came to Cambridge with a decade's experience as a parish pastor and six years as a college president.

The year 1953 was different from 1933. It was no longer to be assumed that students were sufficiently content with the world of their elders to follow the obvious patterns. One could not expect the young to assume leadership in the institutions of their elders. Already the revolutions of the sixties were in preparation. I felt a necessity to consult some specialists who knew what was happening.

At that time, I read *The Living God* by Romano Guardini,[4] a Roman Catholic campus minister at the University of Berlin. Guardini describes three distinct stages through which all of us go, and he presents the characteristic shape of our idea of God for each stage. The first stage is childhood. Here provision of food, clothing, and shelter is looked after by the parents. It is not hard to imagine God on the model of one's parents, as a pure provider and protector. This gives us freedom to experiment, to live for whole periods in the world of play as we try on for size whatever we wish of the adult world. All the time our idea of God as parent fits.

The second stage, of adolescence, starts when the child looks a little askance at the parent. One gets the feeling that the image of Dad as the man who could lick any parent on the block has subsided; Dad has fallen in the human ranks. At the same time, the adolescent feels an urge to move out and explore in freedom. Providing and protecting no longer extend their meaning into immediate experience. Now the idea of God has to take in every idea and ideal, every advance. God can only be Ultimate Reality. It is no accident that Paul Tillich was so popular with young people. His God was Ultimate Reality. On the other hand, while adolescents are striving for the pure ideal, they are constantly measuring themselves by the self's performance. Since the self's performance is always rather puny and insignificant when measured by the ideal, the gap causes frustrations for the adolescent.

That cannot last forever, though. The time comes when one has to choose one of many occupations, one of many possible mates, one of many living places; one "settles down." One becomes an adult when one discovers that the meaning of life is concentration upon this new sameness, when one discovers the joy present in the small things of daily living. In this, the third stage, a sort of second naiveté develops. One returns to the model of God as parent, but as parent stretched in meaning by the adult's experience of parenthood. In other words, one returns to childhood's naiveté but with an adult's meaning—somewhat like moving from the literal meaning of a term to a poetic metaphor.

Guardini's scheme was attractive to me because at that time I was coming into my second naiveté. I was reading a great deal in Evelyn Underhill and Baron Friedrich von Huegel and had inhaled the sacramental character of things as the basis for adult life. My anxieties were growing, though, that we were moving into a period when the changing society would throw the normality of this view of adulthood into confusion. Too much was going on in the fifties that had portents for the future. As we shall see, the definition of adulthood is an open question—even in our time.

Guardini's scheme was parallel to that of many Protestant ministers but with a strong sacramental strain that I found attractive. It formed my overall expectations for a good period of time.

A SURVEY OF STUDENTS

By the time I had been in Cambridge for five years, I had become eager to have some spiritual map of the journey the average Lutheran student makes in meeting the challenges of college life at Harvard and Radcliffe. As a minister, I would usually see the students for a short time on Sundays when they exhibited the "religious" dimension of their lives. Yet my concept of faith requires that faith function within the very stuff of life. For the college student this means life in dorms, commons, classrooms, extracurricular activities, social transactions, and times of aloneness. In fact, the students' faith has to do with their essential trust in God to lead them in precisely these endeavors and situations. To live by faith is to take steps in faith on each of these stepping-stones, confident that the God of the future has grasped one and is pulling one forward.

A colleague reported that he had just reviewed the results of a questionnaire he had sent to all the students who were registered as communicants of his denomination—even the 80 percent he had never met. He was brief with his questions and liberal with empty spaces for the essay form of answer that Harvard and Radcliffe students overwhelmingly prefer, and he said that he received returns at a ninety percent rate.

I decided to make my own start at this, and I sent out three unsophisticated questions:

1. With what religious dimension did you come to college, and what happened to it when you came?
2. What changes have come about in this religious dimension in your college years, and what were the influences?
3. When you leave here, what are you going to do about this dimension?

I quote not from notes but from memory. The questions now seem very unsophisticated. One must remember that sophistication in social-studies questionnaires came in the sixties. Perhaps the results were preordained in the questions.

Ninety percent of the questionnaires were returned. The answers were remarkably uniform. First, all the respondents came to college with a religious dimension formed by the family, the home community, and the church back home. Usually for them church was Sunday school. In the first two weeks at college this religious dimension disappeared. The influences to which they ascribed this were conversations with prospective roommates, bull sessions with dorm mates, and class discussions in sections and, occasionally, in lecture hours.

Second, very little in the college experience revived this dimension. A few respondents gave credit to campus ministers, or to such voices as Tillich and George Buttrick and a few professors who happened to hit a religious theme. For most, however, there was no noticeable preoccupation with religion—at least not in the mainstream of their college experience.

The final question brought the most revealing answer in almost every case. The respondents reported that after they left college and had a family they "would teach their children the same myths." Now that *could* mean that these students were sophisticated enough in their understanding of the term "myth" to use it to refer to the great stories forming our cultural world—stories that give shape to our experience and morals. My knowledge of the students involved, however, was that most of them had never been exposed to sophisticated interpretations of myth. Instead they simply accepted the Comtian description of the periods through which we have progressed: periods of magic, religion, and science. In their understanding, myths were simply stories hanging on from the past like fairy tales. Their comments suggested that they would graduate without any appreciable techniques for teaching their children religion and morality, apart from the tales of Christian lore.

Five years later other students were questioned, and their answers paralleled our first results. Obviously, we needed a more sophisticated instrument, which could test not what students identified as their religious dimension—because that was almost nil for some—but their main stance in the life currents of the university. That instrument was to come to us in the immediate future.

I use the term "faith" where we begin to reveal the intellectual and ethical development of college students. The faith I refer to is what might be called fundamental faith or primary trust in life. Wilfred Cantwell Smith has shown that such a basic trust is at the heart of the term for faith in all the great religions.[5] It is a fundamental human quality—the essential quality supporting our strides on the pathway of real living. Our own Christian faith is brought forth in answer to God's initiative in Jesus Christ. The good news grasps us as it comes from the future and pulls us into growth and new life.

THE PERRY STUDY

The United Ministry at Harvard/Radcliffe is a free association of Christian and Jewish ministers who have responsibility for students of their faiths at the university and who are willing to work together in mutual trust. As such a voluntary group, the United Ministry can provide a meeting place where matters of common interest concerning ministry and university can be discussed

In the early fifties, we invited William G. Perry, Jr., head of the Bureau of Study council, to meet with us. He was the person in the university closest to students' problems of academic study and growth. Widely educated, broad in his reading, a Renaissance man in the modern day, he stood astride the latest discoveries in cognitive development.

Perry told us of a foundation-funded project he was commencing to study the development of Harvard and Radcliffe students. The study was to involve a good number of students chosen in their freshman year and followed through their four-year course with open-ended taped interviews each week. The interviews were meant to show where the students were in their classwork, home-work, social life, dorm life, athletics, and extracurricular activities—in their whole living. Then the study staff would go over the tapes, looking for patterns. If significant patterns were discovered, the findings would be written up in general form in a manual. The manual produced would then be tested against the tapings of the next four years. If the early patterns were confirmed, the project would have amassed empirical evidence of how selected students had changed step by step in these particular years. That would be a research result with few precedents, and it would be a step toward real knowledge.

The Perry study was carried out during an exciting time. Human studies were just beginning to emerge as respectable disciplines in the university, and their impact was to grow during the last phases of the study. Jean Piaget's study of cognitive development was be-ginning to affect the academic world, Erik Erikson's studies of young people coming to their sense of identity was influential, and the theology of Paul Tillich was intersecting psychoanalytical think-ing. Very soon in the study the researchers found that the intellectual and moral progress of students comes as a rule, not by gradual, imperceptible development but in a context of growing anxiety and resistance that issue in an explosion and thereafter a rebuilding of the students' surroundings.

It is as if we create bubbles of assumptions and limits within which we can reside comfortably. Inside the bubble we grow ac-customed to routines and habits and postures. We organize from the center out. But as we approach the outside of our bubble, we find things illogical and unsystematized. At the frontier we live in anxiety that the bubble will break, and we are self-defensive. Our anxiety is enough to make us shrink from progress, and we may try to escape to a safer place or to temporize for a bit. Usually, however, if the challenge is constant, the bubble will explode, with consequent distress to the self it houses. Here there will be a move into a strange new world with different horizons, and again we will build a bubble and settle down—only to be challenged to growth again. In each change, though, our experience is important, as it is gathered up and integrated by us.

The Perry study was conducted quietly during my first years in Cambridge, and the results of the first series of interviews were written up in a manual. This manual was then corroborated by the second series of interviews. The study as a whole was presented in a fascinating volume by Perry entitled *Forms of Intellectual and Ethical Development in the College Years—a Scheme*,[6] which came out in 1968, just when disorder was breaking out in the universities all over the country. Students were trying to take undivided command of the intellectual process. How then could a study of an establishment institution in quieter times have anything at all to say to the new student? Such a good book could hardly have come out at a worse time!

But the seventies were much friendlier to the Perry study. Word of it got to college deans, and many a counseling office was reshaped by its influence. It stands as the grandfather of succeeding psychological studies and, as time goes on, towers above most of them.

Following on the heels of Perry's work was the work in moral development by Lawrence Kohlberg, of Harvard's School of Education. This had wide-ranging influence on Catholic parochial-education theory. Then the continuing work in human development at Harvard was summed up by Robert Kegan in *The Evolving Self*.[7] And it all came to a climax in the recent work of Sharon Parks, *The Critical Years*.[8]

The last fifteen years of my ministry were intertwined with thinking in this critical field. Perry's theory enriched my practice a great deal. We must, however, avoid the temptation of considering Perry's scheme to be *normative*—a rule to be followed—for all college students. Perry himself is always careful about this. All he claims is that his study yields some empirical results concerning a certain number of students at a particular place and time. He is careful to explain his techniques in detail and to acknowledge his assumptions. He simply encourages others to engage in like studies.

THE PERRY SCHEME

Perry starts with an assumption—a judgment he wants all to realize. He believes it is a good thing for a person who is brought up in a province—as all of us necessarily are—to be deeply exposed in a university to the world in all its plurality and relativity. He expects the university to show us all sides of the world in which we must find our own way. We are not born in some universal dimension; we have to be born in a particular, limited place. Therefore our journey must be from particularity into the one shared world, with all its diversity. Perry assumes that it is a *good thing* to make this journey. I share his assumption, but I readily agree that not everyone does.

Perry describes the university as a space where change occurs rapidly—so rapidly that we can see change from day to day. The university is a field of electricity where the current is turned up high. In this field, we move through three large phases. We start with our home position, the province where we have been trained to see things in a simple right/wrong way and in absolutes: things just *are* that way. We then move into a world where everything seems to be relative to other things and where there are strident and opposing claims made by various groups. We are liable to feel ourselves overcome at first in this area. Finally, though, we somehow come to find our enduring selfhood here, discover our own style of operation, our own choice of community, and our own commitments.

Perry finds nine stages of development in all, three in each of the three large phases:

First Stage. Things seem to us right or wrong in a definite way. We think in terms of absolutes. Mathematics, where an answer is either right or wrong, provides the model for our knowing. There is a sort of life fundamentalism here.

Second Stage. There seem to be many answers to questions, but we have not yet grown to appreciate that this is as it should be; we still think that every answer is either right or wrong. We are likely to complain that our humanities professor does not know his subject as well as our math or physics teacher. The trouble is with us, who are now working in a human world that is alive and wiggles.

Third Stage. Seeking for a definite answer but not finding it, we believe it will turn up just around the corner, in an area not yet explored. Religious people are familiar with this in the position of the "god of the gaps": when evidence for the existence of God has not shown up, we expect to find it in an area we do not yet know. The pluralistic, relativistic dimension of reality is still not recognized.

Fourth Stage. We move to a general understanding of relativity and plurality. Maybe there is not any right answer after all, we think. Maybe there are many answers and we will have to find our way to a method of gathering them, judging them, and deciding. We are losing our innocence; more and more doubts appear. This is the stage of sophomore agnostics.

Fifth Stage. We come to the recognition that relativism is here to stay and that there are different claims to the truth. Nothing stands firm in itself, it seems. This stage is what religious people call the dark night of the soul. Parks calls it the time of "shipwreck," because what has carried one this far sinks to the bottom. We seem to be the "victims of the masters of criticism and suspicion." It is so painful to stay at this stage that we cannot bear it for long. Either we go on to the next stage or we slip back to a prior stage.

Sixth Stage. When everything around us has collapsed, there is one reality that remains: our own identity as a person, our history and our future. The Erikson question of identity arises: Who am I? We answer the question by examining who we have been and by pondering what room there will be in the future for what we have been. This leads to a reconstruction of our own personhood from materials from the past and the present.

Seventh Stage. We try to orient the self in our new relativistic and pluralistic world by making a commitment in behalf of some interest. This is basically a social stage in which we move from personal struggles of self-identity to finding ourselves in action in the group.

Eighth Stage. We experience the implications of a commitment. We explore the subjective and stylistic issues of responsibility within the social context. Often this means joining an organization where routines and responsibilities are a part of daily life; we find ourselves in these routines as in a style.

Ninth Stage. We affirm ourselves in our commitments and in a style unfolding. The future remains open, but we have attained a style of operating that is effective.

It is in the last three stages, the adult stages, that we seem today to be weakest. In the years since the Perry study, many young people have had trouble finding social ties capable of leading them into adult life. A whole generation of students opted out of the adult world. Though there was a remarkable return to normality in the early seventies, some of the earlier uncertainties about our cultural stability still beset us. I will speak of this later.

In looking at the whole pattern, we cannot help seeing that it traces the development of our whole style of being. This is more than just an intellectual and ethical journey. It is in every way a venture of faith. We start in a land where we parrot our community's faith, move out into a land that challenges every belief we have, and then are led into the land of walking by faith in our own identity and style. The pathway is in every step biblical: the land of Egypt, the wilderness, and the promised land.

Perry notes that not everyone has to go through all the stages. In fact, different levels of a person's being may be at different stages. Too, there are students who temporize and maybe leave college for a chance to "get their head together." Still others will forgo full growth and will be content to live at a stage closer to the home base.

My own experience of the constant oscillation between frontier and home base further complicates the picture. Thus, even the person who has come out into the sunshine of the seventh or eighth stage returns periodically to the home base, but usually to the base as rethought by the experience of going through the stages already reached. But the oscillation between frontier and home will always be there, and that should develop in us a deep empathy for fellows who are at earlier stages of the journey.

As I have said, it is in the last three stages that we seem today to be weakest. But it is also true that the scheme itself seems to be weakest in the last three stages. These stages did not receive the same empirical investigation that the first six did. But since the Perry study came out, there has been a serious concentration on this later period. The developmental phase involving "young people," those beyond adolescence, is now getting its due.

Parks bases her *Critical Years* upon this later research. As a campus pastor, Parks was an early disciple of Perry, using his scheme in her counseling as a chaplain. Since then she has done doctoral work in the field, working with Kohlberg and Kegan. She has found that two critical needs of young people are for charismatic mentors or models who can exhibit a new style in a new world, and for communities dedicated to experimentation in new styles and shapes of life. Her work seems to leave the future open concerning what may eventuate.

I resonate deeply to this emphasis, chiefly because I am beginning to feel that our Christian faith is one that grasps the good news coming out of the future toward us. The good news pulls us through the latter stages of development toward a future we have just tasted—without fear. It stimulates that elementary faith in which Abraham "went out not knowing where he went, but only that God was with him."

THE SCHEME IN
CAMPUS MINISTRY

As I reflect on the history of campus ministry these seventy-five years, I find it intertwined with the scheme of student development. First, for a long time the university-ministering church tried to provide a home away from home for students, to be a church that exhibited all the characteristics of what students had experienced in their home church. It was not hard to be successful in this. The problem, though, was that usually the university-ministering church took no part in the work of the university itself or in the growth of the students' intellectual and ethical experience in the university world. Often the church set itself *against* the university world and tried to protect students from overexposure to it. Even today, the churches that provide a home away from home are usually full. As we have seen, *all* of us like to return home. A number of us seek to escape from the perils of learning; still others enjoy turning the religious dimension into a perpetual stage of sharp right and wrong. We find around us large numbers of students gathered into tight fellowships with absolutist views. Where individual students from such groups encounter and react to the university world, both campus ministers and college counselors are seeing students with accentuated problems and crises. They are caught in between.

A clear recognition of the process of faith development may help a counselor sort out which are problems of authority that must be outgrown and which are simply the evidence of a conservative mind. I in no way want to argue that in everything there has to be progress from a conservative to a liberal point of view. My own conservatism is based largely on my progress to the sixth stage, where I rediscovered my roots and reappropriated them in a conservative way. I trust that others may do likewise.

Second, in the Protestant campus ministry, unlike the churches that sought to be homes away from home, there was, as I stated above, an early acceptance of the university world and the growth that it entails. Campus ministers were chosen who were inveterate inquirers and doubters. They could move freely on campus, engaging students in conversations and stimulating their thinking. Unencumbered with the church as institution, they could enter into student life with its emphasis on freedom from the establishment. Many of us owe a lot to ministers who led us through the "masters of suspicion." They were usually the ministers who themselves had been through it all and could say from their own experience, "Hey! It's all right! Come ahead! There is a promised land beyond!" But there were also the ministers who had got stuck in the fourth stage and who majored in an agnostic criticism. When the shipwreck of the sixties came, they went down with the ship without learning who they were within the church.

Third, Perry's scheme shows me where I invested most of my ministerial and pastoral life. It was at the sixth stage, where the student—after coming through the "masters of criticism and suspicion"—asks the question, Who am I? Very often students, usually in their junior or senior year, came to me with this question. Because I had found my selfhood largely through the discipline of keeping a journal and using it as a tool in the service of spirituality, I usually started these students off on such a discipline, slowly at first. They wrote down paragraphs on successive days and saw me once a week for guidance in examining their image in the glass of their writing. Gradually I showed them how to move from attention, to connecting, to judging, to acting. This led them to self-identification and the desire to find their place in their societal surroundings. Actually I was leading them from the sixth stage to the seventh and eighth.

The model of a campus church community as a loose association with all the formal characteristics of a church but informed too by the stuff of the university was a great help to me also. For at this stage students are remembering the church in its familiar form. If there is a continuous thread from the past to where the students are and if the church is able to point to what the students can be in a hoped-for world, that will be a great help to them. At this stage, I was assisting in uncovering their roots. The promises of memory and hope were joined together in a discipline of keeping a journal. The discipline of the journal began a discipline of spirituality—something that has been my constant cry for all of us.

Fourth, the findings of Parks concerning the existence of two needs for young people in the final developmental stages—the need for charismatic leaders and models, and the need for experimental community options—are no surprise to someone who has spent twenty-five years in the leadership of an exciting and experimental community of young people. At University Lutheran Church, besides the traditional services of worship and the opportunity for continued scriptural study, two forums were provided each Sunday in which dimensions of the frontiers of life were opened up to the university and wider world. It was not possible for one to come to church without being confronted with the relativistic, pluralistic world. These forums brought forth information on almost every issue one can confront. Members were brought to the point of action, and the channels for further action were opened. The community of faith at University Lutheran Church was actually a community of the sort Parks has found young people need.

But in the wider community there were complementary groups that took the action further. I remember a group of Harvard and Radcliffe students who called themselves Tocsin. A tocsin is an alarm bell that is rung to call the community together to consider a real community problem. The members of Tocsin would canvass the general community for concerns, select a particular one, research it enough to identify those in the community who could serve as resource persons and who were ready to speak, and schedule a protracted meeting—often going through the night—for speakers to hold forth. Before the meeting, flyers would be printed, and the members of Tocsin would descend on Harvard Square, ringing bells and giving out printed invitations. The initial effort of Tocsin was just to get a handle on the complexities of the selected problem and to expose the public to the various views that could be taken in its regard. It was to get attention. The next step was teach-ins—marathon meetings that presented all sides in detail. Intense preparation was needed to match the complexity of the social and national issues that developed in the fifties and sixties and are a part of modern life. Having lived through the succeeding revolutions of the sixties, built as they were on such tireless work, I worry that many today start from scratch and are ineffective just because they ignore the experience of groups like Tocsin which found the handles.

I have reported on the way human studies in my years of ministry have intertwined with my own development of the pastoral office.

That I have concentrated on work with adolescents and young people is obviously because that is where I have served. It is also the area where clear empirical work has been done and we can see what happens, really. But though we see as with a magnifying glass what happens with university students, that story illustrates the changes that take place in all of us. The task of the pastor is to engage people along the way by tying together the gospel and new steps in faith.

MODEL THREE | *The Discerning of Spirits*

SOME MONTHS AGO, I WAS GRIPPED BY A television showing of a "Nova" production by the National Geographic Society called "The Navigators." In the South Sea Islands, where human settlements are sometimes removed from one another by thousands of miles of open sea, there is a need for navigators, since few islands are self-sufficient. Without scientific guides and generally without astronomical observations, these navigators determine where they are and where they should be going by listening to the water lap against the sides of their boats. They listen for the water's sound and intensity and direction, for the waves are the result of island obstructions. The navigators have, by a wondrous discipline, gained the power of reading a hidden language.

To dispel the viewer's skepticism, an open boat was brought to Hawaii to set out on several thousands of miles of open sea with the objective of finding the tiny island home of the navigators. This the navigators did successfully. Their discipline was one that requires half a lifetime of training. Today only the older men are competent. With modern ways of movement, there is really no need for the skill, and the young are unwilling to go through the basic training, so the skill will die with the older men, the navigators. The metaphor stands before me, though, as I recall the film in lasting amazement.

The image serves for my own experience in what is an almost unknown discipline today but one that I developed during my life in the university world. For this world is not staid and stagnant at all but full of currents moving to and fro constantly. Some of the currents are sustained for a period of years in what we call movements. Movements have a life history: they have a source, as well as a period of first springs when everyone is enthusiastic, a period of gathering force, and an adult life when everyone is saying, "Of

38

course"; but then countercurrents break up the movements, challenging their presuppositions but absorbing their message, and finally leading to calm.

In the rising phase of a movement, nothing seems able to stop it, because its genesis is in some truth that cannot be argued. Then come the overstatements, confrontations, unexamined assumptions, the use of the media and political power, and a certain ruthlessness really inappropriate to the university. For the moment, all gives in to the movement.

There is, however, a story reportedly going back to medieval times in the University of Paris. God first created the world, and as the highest point of his creation he formed a university professor and found it good initially. But very soon God detected the rise of pride in this new creation. He summoned Gabriel and asked for his advice. Gabriel replied simply, "Make him a colleague!" Sooner or later every academic movement will have its countercurrent. One can count on that—in time. The problem is that from start to end, a current in the university lasts just about as long as a graduate student's stay. Most graduate students are borne along without having any experience before or after the current came to be. They are completely hoodwinked—as are the undergraduates. This makes for excitement, but it also makes the university church a somewhat perilous place to stay for twenty-five years—particularly if one is to steer a straight course through the waters. One has to develop a discipline of recognizing the currents, of "discerning the spirit."

NAMING SOME CURRENTS

I call to mind successively some overpowering currents I had to deal with in these years. For all of them I had to do extensive reading, pondering, and deciding:

- The explosion of physics and mathematics that brought about the technological revolution of the space age and the Cold War
- The breakthrough in biological studies (e.g., the breakthrough described in James D. Watson's *Double Helix*) and the rush of the brightest minds into biological research, especially that of molecular and genetic biology
- The genesis and growth of a new type of science: anthropology, sociology, ethology, psychology
- Studies in human cognition and in the development of human cognition; Erikson's exciting studies of identity formation

- The confrontation of the races; the civil-rights movement; black power and black consciousness
- The massive effort to relieve poverty; the challenge of urban reconstruction
- Troubling movements against the Vietnam War; draft resistance
- Ecological concerns; antinuclear movements
- The recognition of the problems between the university and the city
- Managerial theory and budgetary reorganization as they affect church structure
- Consciousness-expanding drugs; other methods of enlarging the capacity of human beings
- Moral-development studies and the resulting educational changes
- Problems of medical ethics, especially those opened up by new technology
- Biological technology and its limits
- The women's movement in every dimension of life
- Liberation theology

Granted, this is not a complete list. In every one of the currents mentioned, however, I can recall wrestling continuously with the issues during my stay in Cambridge.

CURRENTS AND THE LIFE OF THE CHURCH

Though there is an ambiguity in the phrase "discerning of spirits," I hope in what follows to give it a living meaning from within my experience. I use the phrase to designate a navigating through the currents of the university world. I have always believed that my call to a university parish singled me out to be the church's representative at this place. As a responsible person, I have felt the obligation to develop skills for my job—and then to report from my vantage point.

The church lives in the same world as everyone else. Currents in the university generally hit the world of congregations with full force five to ten years later. The church is often subjected to the adult movement, the media, and political forces without experiencing the contrary currents that might dissipate the forces. Thus the church often bobs and tosses, and is carried this way and that. When university currents have allowed me to see that this was about to happen, I have felt it my duty to give warning ahead of time.

I made it my habit to report regularly to the president of the church on the forming currents.[1] I was grateful that he usually passed my letter of prophecy on to the church leaders. It would make sense for some observer at the headwaters to have a regular column in the church magazine.

Much has been suggested about the psychological disciplines behind the biblical prophetic message. There seems no doubt that the prophets' innate sensitivity was joined by human disciplines now lost to us. At least the biblical prophets were extremely sensitive, on the one hand, to the human currents of their day and, on the other, to the pathos of God for his people. My guess is that their human disciplines were not unlike those I suggest here for navigating the cultural currents. Though my own descriptions come from the university world where I live, I believe that what I say has the same force for all. Many of the currents that run with full life on the campus eventually move out into every corner of the nation.

THE GENESIS OF A DISCIPLINE

In my early ministry, as a pastor of a large congregation, I found two areas of my life especially worrisome. The first was my own life of prayer: how could I not only carry my pastoral responsibilities of visiting but also find time and sufficient discipline to pray for those I visited? I never seemed to get that problem under control. The second problem was presented by my need for continuously refreshed inspiration in my preaching. I am not a preacher who can prepare one sermon and use it over and over again; I have to speak from my latest thinking each time I enter the pulpit. This doubles, triples the problem of inspiration. How does one reinvigorate the mind? Where do new ideas and pictures come from? How does one clear out the spring of new water? Can one count on a continuous flow?

But back to the first problem. I had problems with the discipline of prayer for a long time. Finally the reason for this became apparent. We all think about prayer—its postures, its habits, its thoughts—from within a general pattern or model, a pattern that was formed in our tradition, that took perhaps two or three generations to perfect, and that we inherit and carry in the unconscious part of our being. I was caught in the particular pattern of prayer handed down to me through the Sunday-school movement and

Pietism. I had models of men and women of prayer which coincided with these patterns. But they were models that did not answer to life in the modern world. And that caused me constant guilt. My conscience was asking me to conform to a pattern that made little sense. The guilt we live under as a result of outdated models is staggering.

It was not till some years later, when I met people schooled in other patterns of piety within my own communion—schooled in the disciplines of orthodoxy, secular piety, sacramentalism, and eastern religion—that I found that other configurations of piety were possible, each with its own tradition. Even if no whole shape made sense, there were bits and pieces of each that did, and perhaps I could put the best pieces together into something new. Only when I realized this was I free enough to analyze the forms of piety, including my own. Once I could do this, I felt myself escaping outside my own shell like a locust and observing the castoff shell. That led me to a new approach to prayer which I shall present later.

DISCIPLINE OF SURPRISE

But it was the second problem for which I settled on a solution first. In order to freshen up my mind, I decided I would keep a journal of surprise. Surprising happenings would give life to my preaching. Anything that stirred my mind I put down in a book. Any quotation from my reading that brought forth an "Aha!" I set down in writing, often quoting whole paragraphs. I purchased a standard journal in octavo form, one I could add to in the same form.

Very soon thereafter, as I was getting to cherish my book and carry it around with me so that nothing that caught my fancy would be omitted, I decided also to chronicle where I was and what I was doing. After all, it is where I was and what I was doing and how I was feeling that brought forth the "Aha!" I would be sure to use adjectives and adverbs in my personal entries to make them memorable.

My personal entries were made in the back of the book, starting there and moving toward the front like a Hebrew Bible. Inasmuch as this material bulked much smaller than the entries in the front, a journal volume usually covered about 125 pages of quoted matter and about twenty-five pages of personal chronicle. Gradually I filled a volume or two—all rather hesitantly and uncertainly. But soon the discipline took hold and became a part of me. The books brought their own rewards. When carrying one, I felt that I was carrying my very own self as viewed from outside my skin; I developed the discipline of memory by rereading what I had in my books and reappropriating it in a different time perspective. After rereading, I sometimes recorded my reflections on what I had written and I projected certain hopes, which I could then also reread and hold before me. The time span that my journal attended to was thus enlarged to include the future. I was enlarging my own life span of consciousness.

In vacant moments, I created indexes. I usually chose some blank pages in between the quoted remarks and the personal material. There I developed two indexes: one of authors and books, the other of topics covered. I found that certain interests were taking shape in my reading out of innate predisposition. Often I was asked to give a short address on some subject I had already researched from many directions in my journals.

DISCOVERY IN THE LIFE OF PRAYER

In the early sixties, I came upon the article "Piety" by R. E. C. Browne in *Theology*. It hit me just at the right time and place. I quote:

> It is always wise, we are taught, to speak little about prayer but to give attention to the things that make prayer possible. . . .
> One of these things, specially for our generation, is the development of flexibility of mind. Von Hügel describes this flexibility as an ability to move from prayer to work and from work back to prayer without the work becoming inefficient or the prayer mechanical. This is a particularly important skill to develop in a society where there is little leisure and little solitude for those who wish to pray. The pious man now is noted not necessarily for the length of time he spends in prayer but for this flexibility which is made possible by his power to work and to enjoy himself without being over-absorbed in what he is doing, or to put it another way, he lives lightly and does not become heavily earnest even in his most important occupations. This way of living is not learnt from textbooks and is best considered as the grace given those who are attempting to live in the light of the Lord's injunction: "Be not anxious . . ." Faith results in a carefreeness which may look very much like carelessness or callousness to an uninitiated observer. Often the pious fail because they overburden themselves with goodness. In prayer, this overburdening is either the result of a rule of life which demands more time directly given to prayer than the fulfillment of obvious obligations allows, or of a weight of intercessions which can turn what could be prayer into a feat of memory or a feeling of guilt at inability to pray for so many good people and causes. . . .[2]

I can remember the shackles of guilt that fell from my shoulders when I pondered the meaning of these words! What was suggested was a new pathway to prayer. It had certain clear characteristics that I have since pursued to my benefit.

First, the development of flexibility—of an oscillation from work to prayer and prayer to work—was of a piece with my own discipline of surprise. I had accidentally stumbled on what could be a new discipline ordering my conscious prayer life.

Second, this should be a flexibility of *mind*. That suggested that formerly our minds were stiff and locked into traditional forms; an effort should now be made to exercise the mind in ways that I had already investigated blindly in my discipline of surprise. This was at the heart of Browne's suggestion.

One can guess the liberating power of this suggestion. It also led me to renewed analysis of the traditional patterns of piety. I came to see that the patterns we have inherited are the products of preindustrial societies and are constrained by their origins. The surprises of my journals, on the other hand, were very much of today, from currents amid which I lived.

At about that time, I was asked to lecture at one of our seminaries. I chose the subject of crisis in piety[3] and made my first attempt to analyze some of the presuppositions most of us have about the life of prayer. It takes some outside challenge like this invitation to force one to analyze one's own presuppositions and prejudices; without the challenge, knowledge about epistemological foundations never comes. My lecture was the snowball that started rolling and gathering snow and speed, bringing me to write *The Christian in Modern Style*. That volume exhibits my own struggles to develop disciplines of the mind. The shape of reformation of the mind that I affirmed there I still affirm some twenty years later. On the foundation I laid there I have come much farther.

DISCIPLINES OF MEMORY
AND HOPE

Many of us have been deeply moved by the testimony of the Jews—as well as of some Christians—who survived imprisonment under the Nazis.[4] Again and again in the stories of the depersonalization of prison-camp life, there are reports of personal attempts by the prisoners to keep their sanity and human personalities. Basic to the disciplines they practiced were their remembering of the past and their projecting of their lives into the future. They celebrated the dimensions of past and future in vivid fashion and thus gained space within which to think of their own identity. But that was difficult when the guards undermined precisely those dimensions. They took away all reminders of the past so that the memory would have no aids: photographs, correspondence with friends, rings, and clothing. Meetings together were banned. Then they operated on the future by spreading rumors of coming freedom, always false. After a number of disappointments the prisoners lost all hope. Once the past and the future dimensions are removed, people lose personhood and become like vegetables: they die.

Former prisoners tell of various disciplines of memory they employed to elicit from the indistinct tapes of their minds details concerning events and people of the past. They would plan their strategies with care, savor the results in celebration, seek to renew them. Then, having nothing in their surroundings to give hope, they would project objects for the exercise of memory the next time—as a tiny space within which hope could work. After a time, the growing human space between memory and hope was enlarged. It provided the prisoners with a sort of objective life out there, separate from prison. Having discovered this method of discipline and its fruits and having seen that our present culture is not that different from a concentration camp in the way it restricts the use of our minds (the concentration camp is like our industrial society but with the amplification turned up high), the former prisoners urged upon us the disciplines they had discovered in their time of great deprivation—the human disciplines of identity.

Of course the disciplines employed in the depths of fundamental human living hold lessons for the church's worship and prayer.[5] It is no accident that those disciplines actually are the church's disciplines of memory and hope which we celebrate as opening a new dimension for daily living. We take the disciplines so much for granted that we are just not conscious of what we are doing. The disciplines of memory and hope in the presence of God are the basic disciplines of our own Christian identity. And they are one whole side of my self-discipline and at the root of my journals of surprise.

ARRIVING AT THE
UNIVERSITY WORLD

When I arrived at the university world, I had filled only about four journal volumes. I had hardly started. In the years since, I have accumulated another ninety-four volumes. The motive for more intensive journal keeping came from reading the currents in the university world. I found that at first I just bobbed on the surface like a cork, always enjoying the latest discovery, and always looking for more. My curiosity drew me to the new-book shelf in at least three libraries, where I became known as an omnivorous reader.[6]

The extent of my reading—always sandwiched between the difficult task of pastoral ministry and life in a large family—eventually brought some depth. I soon found that in seeking to find all sides of a movement, I turned up incipient challenges at the edges of the community, challenges that ultimately moved to the center and tempered the movement's onward surge. This allowed me to survive the "Of course" period and hold my applause until an evaluation came in.[7]

DESCRIPTION OF THE
DISCIPLINES INVOLVED

As I review the process of putting down notes in my ninety-eight volumes, I find that several disciplines played a role. Yet I have to work to make them stand apart as they should.

The first discipline is *attending*. Of course, everyone attends to the surroundings in some way. Yet there are extreme variations in the depth of attending. Just to write down an observation is to attend at a first level of depth. One has to learn how to do this in a way that will bring back the full color in a rereading. It took me some time to understand that I did not need to write an essay or even a paragraph: a few well-chosen adverbs and adjectives would decorate the frame for memory.

That is important because a second step in attending is being able to recall, being able to repicture the original with pristine brightness. Attending and recalling are inseparably linked. One has to select events that are worth attending and remembering and then to portray them so that the effects may be immediate.

There is something in the discipline of attending that makes an imprint on a part of the brain. It is my experience that one remembers not in a flowing process of frames but in single frames. When former parishioners wrote me letters of congratulation on my fifty years in the ministry, each cited certain framed events that stood still in their memories; and I responded with my own recollections in like manner. I find great joy in being able to recall single frames in all the freshness of their setting. If we lose this ability, we are apt to lose an anchor amid the currents of our day.

When I was simply recording what in my reading stirred my mind, my journal keeping lacked much interest. It was rather tedious and pointless with that alone. It was when I started to reread and to reexperience that everything came alive. I had "experience-with-experiences," as Edward Schillebeeckx loves to say. With the rereading and reexperiencing I added notes in the journals to chart the ways in which my moods had changed since the original recording.

Second, I noticed that, after a bit, I began to *connect* things. In a child's number picture, one starts with what are apparently a bunch of indiscriminately placed numbers on a page, then connects the 1 with the 2 with the 3 and so on, and soon there appears the shape of a bunny rabbit, or an owl, always to the child's surprise. Just such surprising shapes jump out at me from the pages of my journals. Somewhere I recorded a note from the New Testament scholar Rudolf Bultmann in which he says, "A person becomes human when he connects things."[8] This I believe absolutely, for I have discovered the enlarging feeling when connections come. Sometimes the discipline of connecting reality brings forth the "Aha!" in capital letters. Right here may very well be the hidden secret of human creativity. This step always comes as a gift; it comes out of the blue! No explanation is possible. And often the "Aha!" of surprise comes when two planes of living intersect for the Christian: the plane of worship, prayer, and study in the language of the tradition, and the plane of human experiences. Schillebeeckx testifies to this in his book *Interim Report,* where he refers to Karl Popper's concept of the "searchlight effect."[9] That is, in scientific discovery often the light goes on when material from the scientific way of life intersects with material from some other way of thinking. As I have suggested in a previous chapter, most of my own life has been lived on two levels: that of biblical concepts, and that of our human living. Just as occasionally with a bilingual person the two languages will intersect and lights will go on all around, so my life has been enriched by the intersection of planes. The two problem areas for me of long ago—the life of prayer and the life of human surprise—though kept separate most of the time, intersect with creative sparks. All this is subsumed under the discipline of connecting.

Third is the discipline of *judging,* of choosing between the different options one has distinguished. Usually we are forced to this
by some outside challenge. Sometimes the challenge comes in conversation, sometimes in confrontation, in needing to lead one's presuppositions up from the dark. It usually comes when we have to
venture out into the current with an opinion. For me as pastor, the
challenge frequently came when I was required to make small pre-
sentations before others. I was always ready to speak on a number
of subjects. My notes fell into pet areas: the civic life, women's
rights, theological education, worship, church music, and campus
ministry, for example. In addition, I was piling up material in order
to converse on the successive "in" subjects in the university. I always
wished to be prepared to go beyond the small talk of the cocktail
hour. Here the readiness of abundant material for judging was called
forth.

The fourth discipline is that of *deciding.* Deciding is necessary if
one is to take a stand. One does that on the basis of judgments,
but deciding is a commitment, it is a move into the open sea. Often
it can be against the main currents, advising an unpopular stand.
Such a stand can be taken only if the ground is well prepared by
attending, connecting, and judging.

A SIMILAR PATTERN
IN LONERGAN

One of the classical theological works of our day is by the late
Canadian Roman Catholic theologian Bernard Lonergan. His
Insight[10] is a large work that sets forth the disciplines of insight as
a basis for a thoroughly human approach to spirituality. His aims
are to put the mind to its best work in response to the gifts of God.
The book is large and complex; I know no one who has read it
through. I have tried again and again, and then turned to books—
there are many—that explain what he has to say. I know the literature well enough to recognize that Lonergan's ideas correspond
with my own discoveries from the experience of journal keeping.
He would call my "Aha!" an insight!

I talk about *attending, connecting, judging, and deciding;* his parallel
admonitions are, Be attentive, Be intelligent, Be reasonable, and
Be responsible. In terms of processes he would list the four areas
as experiencing, understanding, the functioning of understanding
and coming to judgment, and finally, coming to the question of

value and decision. Pervading all these processes and working gradually is, for him, the Christian process of conversion. Lonergan
talks of conversion as like "falling in love" with the God who has
loved one. When one falls in love, the love gradually pervades one's
whole being and makes all one's activities responsive acts in thanksgiving.

Vernon Gregson, in his book *Lonergan, Spirituality, and the Meeting of Religions,* has set forth Lonergan's method of insight as a
foundation discipline toward a universal religious approach to human life. Commenting on the essential disciplines, Gregson says,

> In passing from the level of "experience" to that of understanding to
> the functioning of my understanding and coming to judgment, from
> thence to the question of value and decision, and in allowing the last
> level to broaden out to a being unrestrictively in love, I'm being more
> and more myself. Each level sublates—that is, takes up and extends—
> the preceding in an intentionality that leads toward the final unre-
> stricted being-in-love. A Christian theologian who has really, with
> no cheating, identified all these levels within him or herself and the
> intentionality they constitute, is beginning to experience healing of
> the split between his secular and his religious mind, as the latter op-
> erations are now *felt* as sublating the former's. And his or her religious
> thinking, thus newly appropriated in a universally shared humanity,
> will be newly empowered to *recognize* in culturally very different
> expressions, the same religiously liberated dynamic in other faiths.[11]

DISCERNING OF SPIRITS

I have always had difficulty in unpacking the meaning of the
phrase "discerning of spirits." Instead of facing the difficulty directly
we have approached the task from the back. We have recognized
the predicament first: that of a pastor in the currents of the university
world. We have then described some disciplines that can be learned
in self-defense to open up one's consciousness, bring surprising
connections, force judgments, and form decisions in the midst of
these currents—disciplines that are all the time nourished by a continuing discipline of memory and hope in the presence of the God
who leads us on. We have put this pattern forward as suggesting
the preparation for the discerning of spirits.

Usually one thinks of a discerner of spirits as a lonely, self-sufficient figure, a voice crying in the wilderness, a prophet. I have
instead pictured the discerner of spirits on the model of a South
Sea Islands navigator of a small craft, sensitive to all the waves that
hit his boat. By hidden disciplines he can discern the waves' origin

and their destination. It is that model which most closely parallels my own experience as pastoral leader of a university church in perilous times. The disciplines have been hidden, and I was never confident of my powers. I am still learning, still unraveling the meaning of my experience, and of my experience with experiences. I would be further ahead if at the beginning someone had told me the training I needed. I would guess that is why I am telling this story. We should never set out on such a dangerous voyage without some knowledge of navigation.

MODEL FOUR | *Ritual Eldership*

IT IS A WONDROUS THING FOR ME THAT, after retirement from many years of parish ministry and without any formal training in the subject, I should be chosen by two seminaries to teach worship and liturgy. They must have seen something I could not see. Perhaps what they saw was a practicing leader of worship whose experience they admired and whose ideas were to be trusted. All this was hidden from me because it belongs to the unconscious level of life—the level of actions performed but almost impossible to articulate. How I know that! I had to bring all this to articulation in order to present my first lecture. Now, seven years later, I am still bringing up exciting material from my experience and putting it into words—some of which are just appearing in print.

Recently I read a fine article by a psychiatrist commenting on the findings of Victor Turner, the anthropologist, regarding ritual.[1] He gave credit to Turner for bringing the world of ritual into public conversation in a new way, a way that made sense to his profession. Some years ago, he said, pastors seemed to be trained to counsel persons only long enough to isolate the peculiar character of their problem and to make a referral to some specialist, usually a psychiatrist. When the patient came to the psychiatrist, he simply perplexed that therapist. What was needed was what Turner calls a ritual elder, a person informed in how to perform acts with religious meaning. The psychiatrist suspected that this was so, but did not feel he should suggest how the pastor ought to practice his profession. Until such studies as Turner's, most of us had not thought about rituals this way. We just acted them out unconsciously.

This article brought a sigh of recognition to me. Though I led worship services Sunday after Sunday, using the liturgy of the church, my mind's horizons were not expansive enough to see that

what I did unconsciously in worship applied to the needs of coun-
selees.

Studies of ritual like Turner's are less than twenty years old.
Previously, unconscious corporate actions were the object of anthropologist's investigations only if they occurred in African or
South American tribes. But findings concerning such tribes could
easily enough be written off, for in modern culture we had pretty
much accepted Comte's three-stage cultural progression: from magic to religion to science. We were convinced that we lived in an age
where ritual was passé. It lingered in back corners only—or so we
assumed in our sophistication. Recently, however, anthropologists
have constructed concepts that unearth the place of ritual in our
own culture. Rituals are the patterns of human habits; religious rites
are corporate actions that we perform as part of our human nature
when we are in impossible situations. They have their parallels in
the rituals of birds and mammals, about which we all know from
television nature films.

Rituals are what we do unconsciously when we are at a limit of
life, when the routine makes no sense, when we are up against some
power transcending ourselves. Then all we are capable of is some
traditional action. The action takes over. It creates a world of new
horizons; the action points to new dimensions. We bring the new
dimensions back to our life's problem. A ritual elder is someone,
a little more experienced, who knows what action is necessary and
who can give leadership. It is that sort of person the psychiatrist
sees the need of in our day. He calls for ritual elders who know
what they are doing and what is needed. His earnest challenge to
the clergy underlines for me that a model before everyone in training for the ministry should be that of the ritual elder.

AN EXAMPLE OF A RITUAL ELDER

Just before my retirement we were saddened by the sudden death
of a grandson, on Easter Sunday. Among the many cards of con-
solation we received, one was unique, from a colleague in the ministry. In a short note, we were referred to a passage in *Pilgrim's
Progress* where Christian is on the pathway to heaven. Along the
way, he comes into a marshy place where the path moves into the
Slough of Despond and every step puts him deeper and deeper in

the mud. Christian becomes distraught and ready to give up, but just then there comes to him a faint sound as of someone singing. Listening carefully, he hears a group on the pathway beyond singing "The Lord is my Shepherd." Using his ears to guide him, he follows the sound of the singing back to the path and so comes to solid ground. This was the pastor's message to us: in the time of lonely despair, listen for the sound of voices on the pathway just ahead.

Graphically, then, the picture of the ritual elder is of one on the pathway just ahead with the experience of having come farther than we. Such a one is invaluable in telling us what to do in a limit situation.

A PICTURE OF A RITE

Many who study worship are assigned Ninian Smart's delightful little book *The Concept of Worship*.[2] The reader picks the book up expecting an immediate definition of what worship is. Instead Smart describes what is meant by a rite. He takes a single rite, describes what one does in it, and then makes comments about its various components. He does not take it apart, or it would collapse, for it is only a living thing in totality.

It used to be that we analyzed worship into parts we could talk and reason about. The great change today is that we now consider our social life to be formed of things we just do. The things need not make sense; people do them unreflectively. To describe worship is to describe what people do—to describe the phenomena. The devising of descriptions of what people do is called phenomenology, and Smart takes the phenomenological approach to worship.

The rite he selects is a normal one, if a little out of date in our time: that of a private saluting a lieutenant. The private comes up, clicks his heels, raises his right arm crisply, allowing the hand to touch the forehead. That is a rite. It has meaning. For example, what if instead he had thumbed his nose? That would have done violence to his relationship not only with the officer but with the whole structure of army hierarchy upon which all depends. Instead, he salutes, he does what is expected to strengthen his relationship with the officer (though a junior one) and to give meaning to the whole structure.

Smart sets this forth as a model for thinking about worship, a liturgical act, and he makes suggestions about that act:

1. It is a rite, an expressive deed, habitually done—not talked about but done.
2. It is relational: it enters into a power field of relationships, and it brings forth currents in this unconscious field.
3. It recognizes and contributes to a flow of power toward the Focus. Smart does not use the term "God," because he is suggesting a model of worship acceptable to others who do not use the term. But Focus (with a big *F*) is enough.
4. The whole act breathes a sense of overwhelming and even fascinating power that inspires reverence or respect.
5. It participates in the personal: this whole flow implies that the Focus is personal.[3]

THE IDEA OF THE HOLY

Smart relies on a much earlier study, a classic: *The Idea of the Holy,* by Rudolf Otto.[4] In examining the concept of holiness, of being set apart, of reverence, as the heart of the religious dimension, Otto isolates a feeling that takes over human beings when they are overwhelmed. He calls the feeling the *mysterium tremendum* and finds two sides to it: an overwhelming force, and a fascinating attraction. Think of people on the brim of Niagara Falls: they are overwhelmed at the majesty of the scene, and some are even drawn to throw themselves into unity with the falls. Otto coins a word for the feeling of dread, or holiness: the "numinous," a strange quality that evokes reverence. It seems to have been a natural thing in primitive times for human beings to define some special space where they could imagine the numinous to dwell. Just as children will separate a space for play where there are special rules, so adults will design separate places for special activities. Play is only one step removed from worship. Holy places are for holy rites. Every attempt is made to surround the space with pictures that allow the worshiper to imagine the set-apart, the holiness.

SACRED SPACE VERSUS
HOLY PEOPLE

Christian history has seen a constant tension between polarized teachings: the idea that holiness belongs to the space has been in constant struggle with the idea that holiness belongs to the people.[5]

One can see the tension in Old Testament history. In the movement from ark to tabernacle to temple there was a drive toward setting up a sacred space as the center of religious life—a place where one could encounter the numinous. Then with the destruction of the temple came a crisis. The sacred space was violated, and that brought the people to imagine that they had reached the end of the road. The prophets, however, had prepared the people for this crisis. They taught that, fundamentally, holiness belonged not to a building but to the people themselves, the people whom God had chosen and whom God wanted to respond to the divine call. In the interchange between God and these people arose their set-apartness, their holiness. During the exile, religious life had to center in the people themselves, for they had no temple. The synagogue—or people gathered around the Word—became the center of religious life. When the people returned to Jerusalem, they rebuilt the temple, and holiness was again located in a sacred space as well as a chosen people.

Our Lord accepted this duality. He attended temple worship and taught both in the temple and in the synagogue. At his death, however, he talked of destroying the temple and identified it with his resurrected body. The early Christians had a wonderful chance to reemphasize the holiness of the people. Since they could not build sacred spaces in times of persecution, they met for worship in normal living spaces, but they met as the people of God, the body of Christ.

With the Constantinian era, Christianity came out of hiding and became the official religion of the Roman Empire. Buildings were needed to contain the rituals, which now involved great numbers of people. The church took over the public buildings and started a long era of refining the holy space. The Gothic period, for instance, stands out for the human effort to capture the sense of holiness, the numinous, in sacred space. At the time of the Reformation there was the opportunity for Protestants to emphasize the holiness of the people of God. Only the sectarians, however, applied this emphasis to their meeting houses. In the nineteenth century, particularly in England, there was even a revival of medieval sacred space—a revival that influenced the United States in the early twentieth century.

It was as a result of the bombing in World War II that a change took place in church building. When the buildings were gone the church was still there: it was the people themselves that were the church. With a reemphasis on the people of God as the locus of holiness, a new type of space was required: a place for the people to assemble around table and lectern. The church in the round, or approximations to it, became fashionable.

But the tension has not ended, Harold Turner affirms. New discoveries in ritual studies are reinstating the fundamental meaning of sacred space. In addition, we see that it has been next to impossible to recover a sense of holiness through our emphasis on the people. It has been too easy to sit back and be satisfied with our own community and to lose ourselves in psychological togetherness. Thus, transcendence quickly vanishes, and with it the numinous. Reverence and awe vanish too.

This need not be if we can reestablish a sense of what we do in worship. There are two ways we can go. First, we can try to reach down into the unconscious area of life and put it into words. I have been through this in trying to articulate my own experience as a ritual leader. I confess that this way is fraught with great difficulty. Second, we can seek the assistance of anthropological investigations, of ritual studies. We turn now in that direction.

PERSONAL RECOLLECTIONS

Shortly before I was born the anthropologist Arnold van Gennep published *Rites of Passage.*[6] Van Gennep had studied the rites of African tribes, particularly the rites associated with certain critical points in life. He found three distinct stages of ritual through which the tribe members went repeatedly. Because they did appropriate and traditional things in moving from one level of personal life to another, they always knew when they had left a lower level and arrived at a higher. Thus the assumption of the responsibilities of a higher level was always well marked. Van Gennep labeled the three stages of ritual *separation, threshold,* and *reaggregation.*

Despite the suggestiveness of van Gennep's work, it was quickly passed over. At that time our culture was deaf to ritual studies. We were children of the Enlightenment and used words and ideas to unpack the things we did and the pictures we looked at. Metaphors were thought suitable only for those who could not bare their meaning in clear, logical words. It was assumed that the verbal levels of life were higher than the nonverbal. We had swallowed Comte whole.

THE LITURGICAL MOVEMENT

Soon after I graduated from the seminary I was swept into the early phases of the liturgical movement. This movement, which aimed to discern the actions in liturgy, coincided with the new cultural interest in rite. It received a huge impetus from the findings of Dom Gregory Dix, an Anglo-Catholic monk in England. Dix had come across a previously undiscovered text of an early Christian work (ca. A.D. 225) that had been unreadable till his find. For him the text revealed the shape the Christian liturgy took at the earliest age one could discover. The shape of the Eucharist consisted in the distinct actions of our Lord at the last supper.

In *The Shape of the Liturgy*,[7] Dix laid out seven discrete actions at the last supper, but that number collapsed readily into the recognizable four: our Lord *took bread, gave thanks, broke,* and *distributed.* Even apart from the words spoken, Christians' actions in imitation of the Lord's were at the center of what these believers did whenever they came together. The eucharistic rite was a strong act of identity. Surely words were used, but the words were to accompany actions that were meaningful in themselves, for worship at its heart is what we do.

What appears without life can hold life in abundance. Years ago, when our twins were young, they brought into the house some twig-like pieces with swollen ends to add to the nature museum they maintained in their rooms. Two weeks later, in a warm spell, we found the rooms filled with praying mantises! The cocoons had been left behind.

One thinks of countries where Christianity has been persecuted. Usually the first onslaught is on the verbal front. Preachers are not allowed to preach. That is supposed to remove the obvious threat. The oppressors assume that the ritual is half dead anyhow and that only older people will come to a ritual without preaching. Instead, we have seen in our time that ritual, with its picture language and pointing, is able to nourish faith and can break forth into new life.

In the liturgical movement's emphasis on the actions in worship, attention turned to the actions at Jewish meals of thanksgiving. The tie between the ritual of Jewish fellowship meals and the ritual of the Eucharist suddenly struck us as extremely significant. As in all movements, there was a morphological process. In the early years, when I was caught up, there was a liberating wind in our leadership of liturgy. The actions became important; we believed that they should stand out clearly and that all else was secondary. In that innocent belief, I became a leader in the movement, traveling here and there, talking about worship as action. I occasionally ran into opposition from those who thought of actions as suggesting "good works."[8] My own understanding of worship as action had come from a new understanding of pre-Christian Jewish worship practices, a new look at the worship of the early church, and an acquaintance with discoveries concerning rite which applied the concepts to our modern ways. Nevertheless, many of those with whom I spoke wanted to conduct the battle in Reformation categories. Until both sides can talk on the basis of what exists in this century— in our tradition and human studies—we will argue the old battles and not meet each other. My experience, however, has taught me that, in trying to open up consideration of the actions of worship, I must not forget that there remains a tremendous importance to the verbal side.

In my talks about worship in action I used to employ a model that became rather well known. I imagined us in the position of a boy of twelve invited to visit the president in the White House. What are our thoughts and actions? A natural succession of events takes place: preparation, entering into the presence, listening to the word spoken to us, responding to that word with our offering, the gift to us, our thanksgiving, our life of service. This was shown to be a natural succession of acts, and to be the actual succession in the worship service: these actions are the distinct elements of our worship.[9]

I tried to show that *all* of our tradition in worship should be thought of as simple actions in a traditional shape.[10] The office tradition, the service of the Word, the Eucharist, and even rites of passage can be divided up into traditional shapes, actions that we just *do*. The shapes of those successive actions become the "elements" of liturgy that the church requires of us. The particular way in which these acts are carried out amounts to a "style," and that can be very different according to the talents, abilities, and materials of the particular congregation. A living liturgy contains both elements and style.

SURVEYING THE WHOLE FIELD

Very recently part of my assignment has been to help a seminary seek my own replacement as professor of liturgy and worship. We started by interviewing without a thorough discussion of what we wanted; everyone had an idea based upon personal reactions to what is going on in the church and upon personal private piety.

Traditionally a teacher of liturgy and worship has had intensive training in church history, particularly in liturgical history and the church fathers. We agreed that that was a necessity. Second, it was felt necessary to have someone who had exercised leadership in the liturgy of the church recently. Transforming new ideas into practical usage is an art that the ritual leader must have.

These two necessities led us into our first interview. And that interview stimulated us to draw up a full spectrum of qualifications, consisting of five categories:[11]

1. Training in liturgical history
2. Pastoral experience
3. Interest in the liturgical movement
4. Acquaintance with ritual studies
5. Knowledge of aesthetic dimensions (music, architecture, visual arts, poetry)

Each of the categories had to be argued extensively and convincingly. I believe it is a good scheme.

RITUAL STUDIES: VICTOR TURNER

The new category in our list of qualifications is that covering ritual studies. In the past twenty years there has been a whole body of study concerning myth, rite, and rituals, and their relation to culture, particularly that of today. Among the leading contributors is the late Victor Turner. Turner did his anthropological studies among African tribes. He reached back to van Gennep's *Rites of Passage* of a half-century ago, chiefly because he wished to concentrate on the three stages of rites of transition: separation, threshold, and reaggregation. It was, however, the threshold stage that fascinated him most of all, because of its importance in the rites. In this stage, initiates are taken to the very limits of their life patterns and disengaged from their routines. In Latin, the term for "threshold" is *limen* from which the adjective "liminal" is derived. At the threshold, far out on the margins, the initiate is exposed in ritual to a traditional way of transition to a higher level of personal life—usually with some ordeal. Reaggregation into the new level follows.

On the stage that Turner called liminality, Robert Elwood writes,

> Of [the three stages] the middle stage, liminality, is doubtless the most mysterious. It is the status of the novice during his time in the initiatory lodge, tomorrow's knight at his nocturnal vigil before the altar, the future king being jousted and jeered by his prospective subjects. It is a time of reversal of all customary structures and restraints. The subject is ritually naked and downcast, betwixt and between. But since at the same time this state negates all the restrictions of structure, in a paradoxical way it is an opening of the doors of infinity, akin to that mystical experience which also requires a stripping away of all worldly garb. These two sides, degradation and the plenitude of a *coincidentia oppositorum,* are well expressed in the language which compares liminal states to death, the womb, invisibility, biosexuality, and journeys into the wilderness.
>
> Liminality is originally a process state, a state of transition. But for some—especially when the quest seems endless—it can become a permanent state, a continual calling. This is the meaning of monks and holy wanderers of all sorts, who manifest it to themselves and to the world through special garb and a reversal of ordinary usage in the matters of sex, family, money, authority, and habitation. They symbolize to the community that an opposite of the "natural" is a possible human ideal, that structure can be transcended, or, rather, replaced with an antipodal structure.[12]

In simple words, this means that by a rite of liminality one can be taken to the very limits of one's life, where the daily lines of color, race, sex, and structures just do not matter, and that one can be led through the rite to imagine a community that is not yet. Then, having seen the vision, one can return to ordinary life, and the vision will never leave. Turner grew to believe that liminal rites are not restricted to simple tribes but exist in modern life in our worship and in any actions that take us some breathing distance away, to the margins of life. Indeed, according to him, the move to liminality is the secret for bringing forth changes in our society. Change comes from the margins and from marginal people.

Turner's studies in liminality have given new vision to biblical studies. Robert Cohn, in *Sacred Space,*[13] applies Turner's categories to a reinterpretation of the wilderness journey and other biblical sorties to the margin. He looks for the features that Turner says should be there, and there they are, enriching our interpretation. Victor and Edith Turner have together made a fascinating study of medieval pilgrimage as involving carefully planned rituals of liminality. They have brought the whole process to our imagination in a new way.[14]

Besides developing the concept of liminality, Turner has offered a term for the binding fellowship among initiates to any threshold-journey experience. He could have chosen the word "community." Certainly "community" has a warm, interpersonal meaning. But "community" has too much the connotation of staying put; it refers to fellowship within a staid and structured group. There is nothing in "community" pointing to the quality that is prolonged after a liminal experience. Turner uses the term "communitas" for those who have experienced fellowship in a liminal experience. That liminal experience is always temporary, fleeting. There is communitas in its memory.

For me, "communitas" is an excellent term to use when we talk of the church—a term that has been lacking up to now. In our traditional self-consciousness as the people of God and the body of Christ—both of which we are in baptism—a whole dimension of movement is simply lost. We identify ourselves as the people of God and the body of Christ, and then we want to draw a syllogistic "therefore . . ." describing some final and glorious state. It seems to me that there should be a large Not Yet written whenever we think of ourselves as the people of God and the body of Christ. In baptism we are thrust into a fellowship that is coming to be but is not yet. The use of the term "communitas" restores both the fleetingness of the reality and the fact that we are seized, as it were, by the kingdom coming from the future. Theologians speak of this as being seized proleptically—ahead of time.

At any rate, the words "liminality" and "communitas" are now established in general use. They bring pictures into our religious talk, but pictures that make our language much more precise. They give the numinous quality of liminal experience to our flat conversation. In their ambiguity they reestablish some mystery—that mystery which always lies at the edge of our life bubble and causes both anxiety and reverence.[15]

Some will seek to temper our enthusiasm for ritual studies, pointing out that the studies do not deliver all they promise. Possibly so. We do not know yet. But I have found them very useful in articulating my unconscious life.

FROM MARY DOUGLAS

Another influential voice is that of the anthropologist Mary Douglas—like Turner, a Roman Catholic.[16] Douglas has been a force in restoring the understanding of metaphor in language and, with that, the meaning of liturgical acts. Using the work of the linguist Basil Bernstein on the different uses of language, she proposes that we think of two distinct poles in our language which must always be set firmly and then kept in tension.

First, there is *restrictive* language. This is family language, known only to the family. It is language pointing to specific events in which all the family shares. Nothing further is needed in words; the language points to its many meanings. Of course, the church's language of worship is such restrictive language.

Several homely examples may help. When I was growing up, we were given two cats, which we named Fritz and Flitz. Fritz was all personality; Flitz did not have a shred of personality. In the family, whenever we wanted to talk about a person without any personality, we would simply say, "She is a P-flitty!" That sufficed. Everyone knew what was pointed to. Again, when our children were little, we were invited to a meal by my wife's professor. This professor, an imposing woman from Boston, wore half-glasses on a dark cord attached to her chest. She looked over the half-lenses as she talked to the children with her air of worldliness. The children coined their term for her. She was "sopheur": I guess that is how it would be spelled, for this is the first time it has been written. All of us in the family know what that word means!

Douglas is here describing the ritual language of the church. It accompanies rituals that are simply what we do. The meaning shoots out like rays—to members of the inner family. Even the peasant knows what is happening in the rich liturgy of the Orthodox church at Communion. One is sharing in the heavenly liturgy—the heavenly banquet of the kingdom—ahead of time.

The second pole of language is *elaborative* language. This is language that explains what is going on. It faces not the family but the world. It even unpacks picture language and tries to explain in logical terms what is meant. It must make sense to everybody. Protestant tradition applauds this; Roman Catholic tradition for a long time held fast to restrictive language, especially in the Latin mass. But since the renewal of the sixties, even the Roman Catholics, Douglas complains, are moving toward elaborative language.

Douglas believes that since the Enlightenment, instead of keeping a balance between the two poles, we have moved steadily from the restrictive to the elaborative. If cultural advance necessarily meant moving from magic to religion to science, this would make sense. But as we have seen, there is much in modern thought to challenge this conception of progress. According to Douglas, the movement from restrictive to elaborative language has done great damage. Few people recognize any longer the indispensability and worth of restrictive language with its metaphors. Restrictive picture language is the only conceptual means we have for pointing beyond our ken. In unpacking metaphors, we lose most of their meaning. By moving to greater elaboration we relinquish this meaning and subtly change worship into a way of focusing upon ethical concerns. We come to feel that we have reached the goal of religion in ethical living. Worship is no longer necessary and is turned into moral instruction. Douglas urges a reestablishment of the pole of restrictive language, and then a restoration of the balance between the two.

WORSHIP AND OUTREACH: A PROBLEM

If we are to seek a new appreciation of rite as something traditional that we simply *do,* that will mean a return to restrictive language. But what happens then to the larger world into which our outreach must go? As worship becomes the ritual of the people of God, how do we enlarge our membership? One can imagine the whole religious enterprise breaking up into little monastic communities living in liminality while the world goes on. Or one can turn the problem around and imagine an elaborative outreach where no one realizes the meaning of a liturgical act. This obvious dilemma has caused many congregations to turn their liturgies into a series of explanations—doing just what Douglas fears. Protestants can testify to where in their tradition this has happened. The use of words of explanation has for several centuries turned liturgy into a matter of merely verbal exercises.

In the Roman Catholic renewal there are two kinds of education. Catechetics is the instruction of those who seek to join the church: it employs largely elaborative language for the uninitiated. Mystagogy is education from the inside. It is for the newly baptized as they experience the meaning of church rituals from within the experience itself, from the inside. For Protestants, our task is twofold: to reestablish the inner meaning of rite and ritual, with its restrictive, family language, through actions and words, and to provide some way of outreach, through the activities that our culture finds attractive—singing, reading, listening to a sermon, praying. The outreach might be achieved through a special, elaborative service once a month or through a second, elaborative service every Sunday. But the important thing is that we must reach both inwardly and outwardly.

WORSHIP AND ACTION

There should be some connection between the liturgical act and results in the outside world. The problem lies in identifying that connection. Recently liturgical specialists in the Roman Catholic church and the Jewish communities came together to consider this problem. It was expected that at their conference words would be changed within each liturgy in order to point clearly to the social actions suggested by the liturgy.[17] But in reading the papers presented, one notices a hesitancy to face this issue directly, as though the question had been posed in a mistaken way. One Jewish writer, however, states very clearly that worship should stand in its own right as the act of the worshiper before God. Since the God we believe in is the God of the covenant, of course there is an implied social component. Nevertheless, worship itself carries one only to an "action stance." Any further movement toward social action must be offered by the community in the form of forums, chances to commit oneself, and the like.

The idea of an "action stance" is extremely helpful. In the early days of the liturgical movement, one carried on one's worship in minority situations. The worker priests celebrated in factories; the campus ministers celebrated in classrooms. The context was there, and there was no doubt about the social relevance of what one was doing. But this disappeared when the movement was adopted as the church's worship. Then the context was the traditional way in which worshipers separated their worship from their action. There was nothing to make it abundantly clear that the liturgy should be applied to one's life. The burden, thus, is left with us as ritual leaders to bridge this gap.

In my early ministry, I looked on the ritual elder as largely a bearer of words. It was his duty to convey an intelligible message about the God who is coming to us with his kingdom from the future. This kerygma is the church's treasure. We have trained generations to believe that this is the center of worship. We should not underestimate the power of this idea. On the other hand, today we have experienced a resurgence of knowledge about what we *do* in marginal situations—in situations where we are overwhelmed. We need ritual elders who know *both* Word and liturgical act and who can lead us into a balanced view of them.

MODEL FIVE | *Leadership in the Civic Space*

WE COME, FINALLY, TO OUR FIFTH MODEL OF ministry—of the minister as leader in the civic space. I might have described the fifth model as concerning the minister as civic leader. But then preconceptions would immediately arise. We would call to mind ministers who understand their public roles as guides for public morality, others who regard their preaching as addresses on public policy, and still others who act out the church's program for social action.[1] Though some of this may be expected of a minister, by the parishioners, this is not what I refer to when I use the phrase "leader in the civic space."

CIVIC SPACE: AN AMERICAN PHENOMENON

In using the term "civic space," I am thinking as an American. Perhaps it was growing up in upstate New York, or spending a short time as president of a college in a small American town, or living through the largest part of my ministry in New England that fills my imagination with former days when things were simpler.[2] Citizens met together in town meetings to discuss and decide matters affecting their lives together.

It helped then that the communities were homogeneous and of the free-church tradition. In this tradition, individual Christians voluntarily bound themselves in a covenant with one another and their God. This created the church as an institution. The same Christians voluntarily associated themselves for various other purposes in their lives as citizens. A number of such associations made up much of the public space. The associations served for the training of leadership, for making proposals for the good of the community, for controlling confrontations between citizens, for arguing, for arriving at a consensus, for deciding and acting on a number of community proposals. In the give-and-take, citizens not only learned to live with one another but grew in the various processes involved, all for the common good.

The civic space was the area in which these things happened; it was the area where one could advance beyond private life to matters of common concern in the shared life of village, town, or city. In the days of community homogeneity it was natural for people to expect the minister to accept some of the leadership.

There are opposing patterns that immigrants brought to the American scene.[3] Of course, in the first generation, and often extending into the third, immigrants stuck close together in ethnic neighborhoods, with the church speaking out for their needs. The immigrants' concerns were, understandably, to protect their rights until they were well established in the new land. With continued immigration into our day there are still a large number of ethnic enclaves. Patterns of church and state from continental Europe have complicated the simple New England pattern. In the immigrants' homelands, government bureaucracy and church inner-mission agencies often filled the public space. Individuals had no opportunity to speak out or to develop into leaders in the civic space. Indeed, the very term "civic space" is foreign to many immigrants. Often in their homelands it was helpful just to know someone in the bureaucracy who could open channels.[4] From this source comes the climb of some immigrant groups to public positions that will open the largess of the public sphere. Much in our political techniques devolves from this expectation.

The variety of types in our communities today assures us of pluralism. The American city has become a complex place. The dream of returning to the civic space of long ago is unrealistic. Yet, I would argue, this country retains much of its democratic heritage and an abundance of voluntary associations within which there is room for leadership development, the proposing of issues, discussions, confrontations, procedures of movement, consensus decisions—all those life processes a community needs for wholeness. Moreover, nowhere in the world can we see and move among such a variety of people from different religious traditions. We should want our minister to be able to move in this space, for it is our everyday world. It helps the minister broaden contacts, sharpen the message, warm the heart, encourage new movements. We want a leader in the civic space.

In discussing the other four models, I was borne along by developments in the fields of human studies. The civic space was almost lost from view. There are few who dare to involve themselves; they do not have to. But it is from long involvement and experience that I came out into this large space, a space where I have some of my best friends, a space where one sees the full dynamics of community life. Therefore it is with no apologies that I wind my tale around my own experience.

PERSONAL EXPERIENCE:
A BIG CITY

My first parish, of about one thousand confirmed members, was on the outskirts of a large city.[5] Almost all of the congregation lived in recent housing developments around the church. Another two Protestant churches and a Roman Catholic parish shared oversight of the residents of the tract. We had no contact with the political arm that shaped the community's life. That came from "out there somewhere." The political dimension did not appear in the daily lives of the laity. They were simply satisfied to carry on their private family lives without the thought of the larger city. They *did* want sewers though, but they were willing to wait, afraid of the assessment.

The church itself took up the time and attention of its members. The building bustled with meetings. My ministerial life was bound to the church. The church members closely observed my family and me. They had little else to watch. Of course, the life of the people was reached by larger concerns. The depression had closed the knitting mills that formed their livelihood. In those days, we just accepted that fact and tried to cope with unemployment. Anger against the owners was the furthest thing from our minds. Sunday-school classes were asked to bring canned goods and clothing to the church each week. A small staff, with sealed lips, saw that the goods were distributed. Any outreach we had toward city problems used the channel of our denominational inner mission. We thought that the people there, somewhere else, would be our voice in city deliberations.

PERSONAL EXPERIENCE:
A COLLEGE IN A SMALL TOWN

My second experience was very different. I became a president of a small two-year women's college in a small southern town.[6] The college was the cultural center of the town. My work mixed me with business leaders and the citizenry at every point. I joined the Kiwanis Club, and was active in the Chamber of Commerce. I organized all the volunteer agencies under a United Fund banner and thus received the Man of the Year award.

Our college was under the state law segregating educational facilities. On one occasion the blacks in town came to me and asked if their community could use the college gymnasium for evening games. Though this gym was attached to our dormitory, I gave permission and spent a few anxious years seeing that there was no publicity and that all precautions were taken. I cherish the memory of the testimonial dinner the black community gave me when I left the college.

The shape of this civic space was obvious. All sorts of things are done together; in fact nothing is done without being together.

PERSONAL EXPERIENCE:
A SOUTHERN CITY OF
ABOUT ONE HUNDRED THOUSAND

My third situation was in a city of about one hundred thousand inhabitants.[7] The divisions of the community brought the population of the civic space down to about twenty thousand, since the black community of about fifty thousand was entirely separate and a "poor white" community of maybe twenty-five thousand was largely ignored. The actual civic space where decisions were made consisted of the middle- and upper-class whites.

That was due to my training, though. I found this small-town space naturally. I joined the Kiwanis Club, helped organize a Boys' Club, and was active in the Boy Scouts. I took as a special project the woeful public library in a museum building, and organized a Friends of the Library. This organization alerted the political world to the needs of the library and caused a fine new building to be erected. My primary interest was that a public library offer books in the religious dimension of life.

During this time the government by fiat took over two counties across the river and claimed the land for the Savannah River Plant of the Atomic Energy Commission. A massive movement of thousands of families took place, and then of thousands of workers coming in. It all created mammoth social problems for our community.

Looking back from our consciousness of social action today, I marvel that no voices were raised in protest against the whole project. We simply accepted its necessity, accepted our part in the new endeavor, and were grateful that we were now on the map. We tried to care for the wanderers in our city, establishing a Traveler's Aid Society and bringing in denominational assistance in extending the church's missions.

Here was a different model, but still a simple one. It was really a model of a small town upon whom a large social responsibility is laid. The community responded well to the new challenge, but the compromises that kept almost three-fourths of its citizens out of the civic space still persist.

PERSONAL EXPERIENCE:
A COMPLEX PATTERN OF PLURALITY

My last move was to a city of similar size.[8] It was crowded into a slice of land across the river from Boston. On the other side of the city, pressing its back, was a city of about the same size. It is often considered one of the most crowded cities in the nation. It was really a part of Boston, but again it was not. It had all the problems and divisions of a great city. Yet it had its own institutions to work with and was allowed its own civic space. I found within this civic space some of the most rewarding experiences of my ministerial career.

In the eyes of most, Cambridge is a city with an educational focus. Harvard and the Massachusetts Institute of Technology hold a good part of the land space. Several large industrial and business complexes occupy another space. And then in defined sections live a heterogeneous population of Irish, Italians, Polish, Portuguese, Nova Scotians, Haitians, and Latinos, as well as old Yankees. Most are blue-collar workers, though in recent years a good number have become lawyers, politicians, doctors, and professional people. From immigrants to professionals, they are all on the way. To my astonishment, when I became involved in the civic space I found very few academics there. Most of them live in other communities, where I hope they serve in the civic space.

The city is divided into large Roman Catholic parishes. Very much like my first parish, each serves a specific geographical constituency. In addition, the Roman Catholics have some ethnic parishes using and preserving native languages and customs and serving the greater Boston area. Protestants are hopelessly divided: black and white, evangelical and liberal, Central Square (blue collar) and Harvard Square (more academic). A few of the Protestant congregations are islands of traditional ethnic but Anglo-Saxon background complete with their secret societies. Others are simply centers for worship, their members living in outlying towns. A few, however, are serving well in a geographical area, furnishing leaders for the civic space.

It was into this complicated scene that I came and within this scene that I spent twenty-five years of ministry. In the closing years of this ministry, I was active in the civic space.

GETTING ACQUAINTED: SEVEN YEARS

When I confess that I spent twenty-five years in one parish, sighs come from many hearers. Long pastorates are not supposed to be good for the church. Maybe they are not, but they are good for the community. One has the chance of doing hardly more than getting acquainted in seven years—the span of the typical pastorate. It took me that long.

My first step into the community was obvious. I looked up the Ministerial Association, a band of ministers who voluntarily meet together for their mutual enrichment and for the good of the community.[9] In those days, out of about fifty-five possible members we had about fifteen sharply divided between the Central Square and the Harvard Square clergy. We showed some unity at Thanksgiving time: that was hard enough.

For a period of two years we decided to devote our meetings to a series of reports from the various ministers on their congregations. A list of questions was given to be answered in writing, and there was much discussion. It gave each pastor an opportunity to pour out his troubles and successes. The picture that was formed was of a small group of congregations huddling in defense against the city. In only three congregations was there any idea of what was going on in the political realm. Very few members of the congregations served on the boards of agencies.

One endeavor of the ministerial association that caught my attention and energies came out of a meeting to which we had invited a beleaguered school-board member to report to us. It was at a time when politicians had their eyes on school appointments for their friends and were manipulating toward the kill. After listening to the board member's sad report, we asked what citizens could do. He replied simply, Keep your eyes open and tell others what you see.

That started me in keeping a log of newspaper reports of school-board minutes, in mimeographed stencils. About six months later the League of Women Voters, who were trying to oppose the politicians, asked me for our log, and we duplicated it and encouraged discussions. We won. That taught me the importance of citizens' monitoring what goes on and focusing on the progress of an issue. Politicians count on weak memories and short attention spans. They are masters of timing. To serve in the civic space one must *attend*.

TENTATIVE INVOLVEMENT:
NEXT FIVE YEARS

My next experience was in serving on various boards of agencies: the Camping Society, which arranged scholarships for the city poor to outdoor camps, and the Family Society, a casework agency for family problems. Financial necessities limited these agencies to working among the middle class and working poor. I got a good look at the earnestness and competence of trained workers, and I gained experience in running a voluntary agency, which helped my own style of congregational leadership. Here I found a number of fine citizens who were willing to give their time and energy to the limits that a board member can. They were really involved for a time, and then left the board to rest awhile.

One effort I took on by myself: to set up a Committee on Fair Housing both to help blacks find housing and to pressure the bureaucracies toward attending to fair housing practices. I recall a particular explosion in my committee at one meeting. A black real-estate broker—usually quite quiet in meetings—burst forth in anger at a white real-estate broker on the subject of discrimination. I had never heard an honest-to-goodness confrontation before. All my work previously had been among those for whom civility and Robert's Rules of Order took priority. This was a preparation for the emotion I was to hear later when I entered the public sector.

DEEP INVOLVEMENT:
THIRTEEN YEARS

My step toward deep involvement was my own. The period was the midsixties. My friends in the campus ministry were in the civil-rights movement and the peace movement. I was convinced that if I could not work out race relations in my own community I should certainly not travel to Selma to demonstrate. I took my place as a board member of our Cambridge Community Services seriously. This was a community council of representative agencies from both the public and private sectors. It was the closest thing Cambridge had to a genuine community council. Only the poor were not represented. I accepted a place on the executive board and after learning the routines and problems took over as president for a lengthy period, during which the executive director left. During the vacancy, and then with an energetic new leader, we faced together the birthing of the process whereby public agencies received poverty funds in millions of dollars.

This brought me to membership on the executive board of the Cambridge Economic Opportunity Committee—a "Cap" agency[10] to set up community centers, develop job-training and youth opportunities, and generally to raise the sights of the poor. Thereafter we put in an application for funds for a Model Cities project. And I became a member of the board governing this project. In these two endeavors I was ushered into a new experience. The boards consisted of representatives of the whole city (among whom I was one), representatives of the providers of services, and representatives of the resident poor. Actually, and to the failure of the programs, the poor came and dominated the meetings. The other citizens and the helpers gradually disappeared. After all, who can take shouting and screaming meetings that start an hour late and move into the early morning? I ended up taking earmuffs and putting them on when the shouts began, for a note of comic relief when it was needed. Too many had seen only the models of their city politicians and thought they should imitate them.

Unfortunately, we were not ready to understand the emotional dynamics that would operate among the poor when they were trusted to pull themselves up by their bootstraps. There were jobs available that any board member would have liked, yet if the board member had applied, it would have been necessary to end participation on the board. The next best thing was to lobby for a friend.

The bureaucracy hired to carry out the programs allied itself with the poor residents, and together they ganged up against the citizens at large and the helpers. The result was chaos.

Yet I saw many a resident start out vocal but inarticulate but gradually rise to leadership in board discussions and then move on to political leadership. How dense some of us were! We thought that this was the chance for the poor to imagine what they wanted. We organized meetings for this purpose and were surprised to find out that the poor dreamed of their garbage being collected, their streets being cleaned, ordinary routines being extended their way. Anything more is born of middle-class affluence. It is the rich who can dream the most.

In this period, I got used to confrontation as a technique. What I had experienced with the black real-estate man now appeared to be a regular part of the process of self-expression. At first came the embarrassment of the howl. People who have been held down so long should be expected to howl. After the howl the inner examination of our presuppositions is possible, and after that, conversation.

COOPERATION BETWEEN PRIVATE AND PUBLIC SECTORS: TEN YEARS

My final journey into the civic space was spent in leading public boards in welfare and then in mental health and retardation, and in serving on boards in health care. Here I as a citizen and a representative of private agencies was able to lead an effort to contribute something to the massive public sector. First, I was chair of the Committee on Public Welfare, a state advisory committee for Cambridge. We quickly found out that the welfare apparatus was so busy in the area of dispensing funds and services to the poor that it had little real information on how the funds were accepted and what was happening to the poor. We set up committees to monitor the funds and the services they provided, and we reported the results to our political representatives as far away as Washington. We received immediate thanks from the politicians, who were eager to see that the best effect was provided and that complete information was at hand. They were grateful that we could make them honest. The information from us was all they could get.

We were of help in a second area as well. All city ministers are hounded by an onslaught of beggars, usually adept at getting a handout. In the Committee on Public Welfare we designed some cooperation between the churches and the welfare workers. If the churches furnished the department of welfare with a revolving fund of about two thousand dollars a year, the ministers could send beggars to them to interview. The caseworkers would use their expertise to see that those sent were well taken care of. Where welfare rules had to be followed, the agents had often adopted a stiff, mechanical method, but where a fund could be drawn from in the case of an applicant who did not fulfill paper requirements, a human attitude was possible. Through a modest investment from the private sector, we made the face of welfare humane. This very happy result was publicized far and wide.

In mental health and retardation, private citizens were responsible for handling funds in a private corporation set up to enable flexibility in many different programs. The crossover of the private and public sectors brought a changed feeling of human warmth to the services. With workers in these areas I have had only the finest experience. The church cherishes its own servants, but rarely have I met such dedicated servants of human need, so poorly paid yet so dedicated, as in the areas of welfare and mental health.

My last positions were in the field of health care. I served on the Health Policy Board of the city of Cambridge; this board had charge of a large city hospital, a number of clinics, a nursing facility, and other services of public health. As a member of the hospital board, I served on a human-services committee. I also served on a similar committee of the Harvard Medical School. In these committees we had to review protocols of medical research in affiliated research hospitals, some of them world renowned. The committee always consisted of citizens like me as well as of medical personnel and personnel from the various professions.

I looked forward to such service, intending to bring a moral voice to the discussions. In my ignorance, I believed that the church had special moral insights into the medical future and should speak out before it was too late. And I studied hard and long in my books of medical ethics. My experience was an eye-opener. Not only were the doctors on the committee sensitive to moral issues because they wanted to protect their profession but they were usually the most adamant about limiting the risks that can be incurred with normal medical methods. Again I discovered that a concern with morality is shared by a whole profession.

In the area of public health we had a committee that worked out for the city of Cambridge a pioneer agreement on recombinant DNA research which won world recognition.[11] It had always been reported that the secrets of life today are too complicated for the layperson; yet many firms wanted to start their recombinant DNA research close to Harvard and M.I.T. A committee of citizens worked long and hard, forcing the experts to unravel the complexities involved so that safeguards could be set up under citizen control. This was done successfully, and now Cambridge has many firms working under the general agreement that was reached.

My pathway has been long and time-consuming: from first beginnings, when I was learning, to tentative involvements, to deep involvements, to adult leadership in bringing together private and public sectors. It is overwhelming to talk about, isn't it? But over a period of twenty-five years it represents only a constant involvement with deeper meaning, a broader outreach using previously gained knowledge, and a final emergence into the open with a rich, usable experience.

LESSONS IN THIS EXPERIENCE

I have given a sketch of my activities in the civic space over these years. Now I will attempt to list some of the lessons I have learned about work in this space. We must remember that my activities were shared with people of different faiths— Protestants, Catholics, Jews, Muslims, agnostics—persons of other races, of countercultures, in all a plurality of different persons and all working for the common good.

- Viewed from the civic space, the divisions of the religious community appear to argue against giving any credence to a single voice. Indeed where a single voice is promoted, the chances are that it is one that has not shared the civic space!
- The traditional agencies that have served human need in a community are generally not shaped or empowered to respond to new, changing demands.
- Eternal vigilance is necessary on the political scene, and it is tremendously helpful in preserving steady service.
- The frontier between old establishments and new demands is always the scene of confrontation. Confrontation comes as an emotional event. We should expect much emotion in a genuine civic space.

- Some new forum must be devised where citizens, the needy, and those who would serve the needs of the needy can meet. My experience shows that we do not have the answers yet. But the poverty program should be recorded as a starting place for future attempts.
- A marvelous metamorphosis took place in the leadership among the poor. The history of these people makes the poverty movement worthwhile.
- It took about a year from the time of making a proposal for funds—say, for drug treatment—to when the program was approved. Often, during the application process everything had to be changed because of the voice of some immigrant group, just arrived. We had to design open structures and methods for dealing with our ever-changing society.
- Monitoring the effects of funds and services provided by the government was extremely helpful to all concerned, and it was easy to establish monitoring procedures.
- Providing private funds to make the face of welfare humane was a gracious note in what can be a hardened interchange.
- Cooperative decisions on what are difficult moral problems can open up our common humanity.
- Decisions that depend upon both citizens and experts can be made. They require commitment enough to go through a rather long process. The results are worth it all.

A cursory review of these lessons shows that I learned a lot as a minister in the process of leadership in the civic space. I could go through and analyze what each lesson contributed to my overall ministry. But it is enough to show the value of this sort of interchange and the results that it brings in our civic life. For there we meet around a table, each bringing some group's point of view; there are confrontations; each of us has to reconstitute what we think; we learn to compromise and move toward the common good; we try to make a decision or announce a consensus. Certainly a fellowship develops in the process. Following Turner, I would call it a communitas, a fellowship at the margins—a communitas that holds our fellow workers in memory. This is what human fellowship is all about—even beyond the bonds of church. It is a precious memory in my ministry.

There are any number of positive aspects to the American civic space:

- The civic area of our country, messy as it is, provides the field in which leaders arise, issues are dissected and put together, positions are taken and irregularities are focused upon—all in such a way that visible changes take place.
- In the process, human beings are constantly sensitized and alerted, getting to know their neighbors, their leaders, and what those leaders have failed to take into account in dealing with the issues of the day.
- The clinical professionalism of specialized service agencies has been tested and has been changed into a system of rendering services where people live—where the whole person must be provided for and where the whole context of the person's life is taken into account.
- New groups have rejected institutionalization and have learned that some organization and routine responsibility are necessary for efficiency—thus bringing a new type of institution into our community.
- Communications from citizen groups close to human problems are gratefully received by our elected officials.
- There is much room for imaginative movement and for the use of citizen power in the associational and civic space of our cities.[12]

TESTIMONY FROM A GERMAN PRISON

I was much moved by reading the diary of Helmut von Moltke, who was martyred by the Nazis. In it, I found a concern with the civic space:

> I started from the premise that it is intolerable from the point of view of European society if the individual is isolated and only brought into politics through a community which is already large scale. Isolation leads to mass society. In such circumstances, single individuals, when combined, merely form part of the mass. In face of the large-scale community of the state, the only person who can really have a proper share of responsibility is somebody who takes some share of responsibility in a smaller-scale community. Otherwise the governed come to feel that they have no lot or part in events, while the governing classes come to feel that they are not answerable to anybody.[13]

That certainly points to the civic space as a place where a great deal happens despite the confused frustrations encountered in dealing with its daily problems. I find sociologists going into almost religious raptures over the possibilities of events in this space of life.

Thus, John Curtis Raines, in *Attack on Privacy* speaks of personal interchange in the civic space as at the threshold of transcendence:

> The lessons of loyalty, holding to our deeds and comrades while also guarding our personal integrity, the lessons of accountability, or long-range solidarity with colleagues whose judgment we esteem and from whom we gain some objectivity concerning ourselves, lessons of mutual encouragement as well as mutual correction, and those sometimes heavy moments of parting when we must say, "No, there I cannot follow you"—all these rich humanizing experiences are the fruit of our private associational life. Here we gain freedom from the moral ineptitude of idiosyncrasy, the arbitrariness of undiscussed certainties. . . . Meaningful community life breaks open and pluralizes the social landscape. It is an instrument of transcendence.[14]

I maintain that one of the richest models for a minister today is that of a person leading us into the civic space.

Epilogue

Several years ago, at a meeting of the Boston Ministers' Club, George H. Williams, of Harvard Divinity School, presented a convincing paper on the ministry. He claimed that the ordained minister was really the "last generalist," the person for all seasons, a sort of Renaissance person. The minister moves broadly throughout the varied conditions of life and provides help for everyone. Williams spoke in the hope that when all others are deserting this kind of generalism, we would cultivate it because of the need.

My experience confirms Williams's insights. From our everyday routines, it is hard to imagine that there are distinct and specialized roles we play. In some way, our generalism is our joy. We are able to meet a new day with a great deal of freedom in arranging how we shall spend our time—far more freedom than the person in business has. Our reading and conversations must be broad to reach the wide-ranging needs of our members. We are indeed generalists. It took some concentration, therefore, to arrive at the five specific models I have described. Maybe there should be more models that focus on administering, counseling, teaching, and on and on. When I tried to set out some vessels that held the riches of my own experience, however, I found that my experience broke down to five functions: scriptural interpretation, faith development, the discerning of spirits, ritual leadership, and leadership in the civic space. These are precisely the areas in which my own experience intertwines with extremely significant advances in human studies during the fifty years of my ministry. The five roles cry out for leadership today.

The role of the ordained clergy is a matter of intense discussion in the contemporary church. Most of the discussion is spent in looking backward to the New Testament, the life of the early church, our confessions, and our practice in history. But I hope that there can also be some consideration of role models from our very own experience. The testimony here is offered in that hope.

PICTURE OF A WEAVER

Recently an exhibit of Chinese culture at the Boston Museum of Science brought with it a number of working artists who showed off their creativity right before our eyes. Striking to me was the weaver. Sitting on a high seat on the top of a huge loom, with the various colored spools of thread behind him, he busied himself in the most expert way with what appeared to be an utterly confusing interchange of shuttles—back and forth. In front of him, on display was what he had finished, a beautiful and intricate tapestry of color and order.

I am no weaver, but the picture immediately opened up some thought. It was not hard to imagine myself, a weaver, sitting up there on that high seat. The future—for weavers as for rowers of a boat—is coming from those spools behind me which I cannot see. My present is the result of the disciplined expertise with which I shuttle back and forth, the whole activity taking all my working time. The work that has been done then lies before me. At first, it is really not worth looking at. But by the time I am halfway through, it has taken shape, and by the time I am as old as I am now, it stretches out before me—the testimony of what God's grace has done with me in life.

It is also a helpful picture of how I might look at future, present, and past, in faith. I have never been able to project my faith into what the future contains for me. The Christian hope seizes the promises of God and holds fast. But in terms of specifics, it all comes from a hiddenness. The present is always full of routines, of daily duties performed one after another, in some order. The present fills all my time and energy. Simply to do nothing is just to fall apart.

On the other hand, the past—the results of a life of faith and action—shows forth in the tapestry of what has been accomplished. Certainly we should expect this to happen. I have testified to what has occurred in five dimensions of ministry. The results are all around me in my office—in books, papers, diaries—while the memory is constantly moving in the midst of this material, seeking patterns of which I was never aware.

For me, *this is it!* Though I always seek the presence of God in the future and in trust, and though I try to lift up my working hours as a gift, it is in the fabric and design of what has been accomplished that the confirmation comes. *This is it!*

I offer these chapters as a legacy to young students headed for the ministry. I cannot believe that they would want to start from scratch or from empty models they feel unequal to. How much better to hear the voice of a brother or sister on the trail just ahead of them, singing,

> Let the people praise thee, O God;
>   let all the people praise thee!
> Then shall the earth yield her increase;
>   and God, even our own God, shall bless us.
> God shall bless us;
>   and all the ends of the earth shall fear him.

Notes

INTRODUCTION

1. See Brian Gerrish's informal remarks in *Luther's Ecumenical Signifi-cance: An Interconfessional Consultation,* ed. Peter Manns and Harding Meyer (Ramsey, N.J.: Paulist Press, 1984), 95.

2. See Walter Brueggemann, "Imagination as a Mode of Fidelity," in *Understanding the Word,* ed. James I. Butler et al. (Sheffield: JSOT Press, 1985).

MODEL ONE:
SCRIPTURAL INTERPRETATION

1. Not enough has been written about the relation of the Sunday school to the church in congregations of the various denominations of American Christianity. Many of us are living a schizoid religious existence in our practices and our thinking. We have an interdenominational base to a fierce-ly competitive confessional consciousness.

2. For the only treatment I know of the influence of this Bible with commentary, see James Barr, *Protestantism* (Philadelphia: Westminster Press, 1977), 191–207.

3. See Bruce Reed, *Dynamics of Religion* (London: Darton, Longman & Todd, 1978). Reed weaves this concept of oscillation into his analysis of church life. His book deserves wide reading.

4. The New Testament professor was Henry Offermann.

5. This was Professor O. Fred Nolde, later influential in human rights, the United Nations charter, and the World Council of Churches.

6. This was Professor Charles M. Jacobs, the best teacher I ever had, a Reformation scholar, and my mother's brother. He was graduated from the University of Pennsylvania and studied at the University of Leipzig.

7. The document is the *Baltimore Declaration* of the United Lutheran Church in America, of 1938.

8. The church was Immanuel Lutheran Church, Cottman Avenue and Palmetto Street, in Philadelphia.

9. This was Marion College, Marion, Virginia. It is now a part of Roanoke College, Salem, Virginia.

10. See Martin Buber, *Moses* (New York: Harper & Bros., 1958), 75.

11. See my "Bi-lingual Man: Ministry," in *The Christian in Modern Style* (Philadelphia: Fortress Press, 1968), chap. 10.

12. See Robert N. Bellah, "The New Religious Consciousness and the Secular University," *Daedalus* 103 (1974): 110–15. Bellah has popularized this term, but he acknowledges Paul Ricoeur as the originator of the idea.

13. See Amos Wilder, *Early Christian Rhetoric* (Cambridge: Harvard Univ. Press, 1971).

14. See Amos Wilder, *Jesus' Parables and the War of Myths,* ed. James Breed (Philadelphia: Fortress Press, 1982).

15. Ibid., 2.

16. See Brueggemann, "Imagination."

MODEL TWO:
FAITH DEVELOPMENT

1. My father began his work in the campus ministry by organizing a "students' pastor committee" of the synod in 1913. In 1917 he went to Cornell, where in 1932 he died at the height of his work. I had to wait till I was forty for the call; I then served from 1953 to 1978 at University Lutheran Church in Cambridge.

2. See this story in my *Lutherans in Campus Ministry* (Chicago: National Lutheran Campus Ministry, 1972), 8ff.

3. See Henry E. Horn and William M. Horn, *A Documentary of Lutheran Campus Ministry* (Huntingdon, Pa.: Church Management Services, 1984).

4. See Romano Guardini, *The Living God* (New York: Pantheon Books, 1957).

5. See Wilfred Cantwell Smith, *Faith and Belief* (Princeton: Princeton Univ. Press, 1979).

6. See William G. Perry, Jr., *Forms of Intellectual and Ethical Development in the College Years: A Scheme* (New York: Holt, Rinehart & Winston, 1970 [1968]).

7. See Robert Kegan, *The Evolving Self* (Cambridge: Harvard Univ. Press, 1982).

8. See Sharon Parks, *The Critical Years: The Young Adult Search for a Faith to Live By* (San Francisco: Harper & Row, 1986).

MODEL THREE:
THE DISCERNING OF SPIRITS

1. For the first fifteen years of my stay in Cambridge, the president of the United Lutheran Church was a dear friend, Franklin Clark Fry. He sent out pastoral letters monthly, which we were supposed to keep in a furnished loose-leaf binder. I hope the libraries have kept the letters.

2. See R. E. C. Browne, "Piety," *Theology* 65 (1962): 320ff.

3. See chap. 2 of my *Christian in Modern Style*. This was the Swope Lecture at Gettysburg Seminary.

4. See Bruno Bettelheim, *The Informed Heart: Autonomy in a Mass Age* (New York: Free Press, 1960).

5. I was swept up by these thoughts when I wrote the appendix in *Lutherans in Campus Ministry*. I was also much beholden to Dietrich Ritschl's *Memory and Hope* (New York: Macmillan Co., 1967).

6. When I arrived in Cambridge, I had to read to survive. First, I had to catch up with theological reading: the parish left little time for that, and I found people who knew more than I did. Second, I went through a period when I read constantly in books that hitched faith to life—Christianity and this and that—until I realized that I was too shallow. Third, I tended to look over the shoulders of research scholars and to read their scholarly articles. All the time I managed to scan the new books that were appearing in the theological libraries.

7. In a lecture at the Gettysburg Seminary, Alexander Schmemann talked about the "Of course" period in a movement, when the media have made certain expressions clichés.

8. I cannot find the source of this in my notes.

9. See Edward Schillebeeckx, *Interim Report on the Books Jesus and Christ* (New York: Crossroad, 1981), 3ff.

10. See Bernard Lonergan, *Insight: A Study of Human Understanding* (New York and London: Longmans, Green & Co., 1957), and idem, *Method in Theology* (New York: Herder & Herder, 1972).

11. See Vernon Gregson, *Lonergan: Spirituality and the Meeting of Religions* (Lanham, Md.: Univ. Press of America, 1985), x.

MODEL FOUR:
RITUAL ELDERSHIP

1. See Robert Moore, "Ministry, Space, and Theological Education: The Legacy of Victor Turner," *Theological Education* 21 (1984): 87-100.

2. See Ninian Smart, *The Concept of Worship* (New York: St. Martin's Press, 1972).

3. See ibid., 3.

4. See Rudolf Otto, *The Idea of the Holy* (New York and London: Oxford Univ. Press, 1923).

5. See Harold W. Turner, *From Temple to Meeting House* (The Hague: Mouton, 1979). The present section outlines this book's argument.

6. See Arnold van Gennep, *Rites of Passage* (Chicago: Univ. of Chicago Press, 1960).

7. See Gregory Dix, *The Shape of the Liturgy* (London: Dacre Press, 1960 [1945]).

8. The papers of the Milwaukee Conference on Action in Liturgy stirred controversy in several journals.

9. I recently suggested the model of the young boy and the White House to a young woman studying theology, and she was turned off immediately. I suggested that she work out a social model that deals with a feast.

10. See my *Worship in Crisis* (Philadelphia: Fortress Press, 1972). The confusion of the sixties brought me to write this book. The first chapters take up some areas of confusion; the second half of the book suggests a reappreciation of the total worship of the congregation, with reference to source, shape, demands of language and space, etc.

11. Personally, I would add another category: knowledge of liturgical theology. The talks between the Orthodox churches and the Roman Catholic church bring their representatives— representatives of the original tradition—down strongly on a point they share together: that theology has its source in liturgy. We are going to have to think this through, especially those of us who would move the other way. I do not, however, believe that we are at that point yet. The field of theology and worship can be handled by shared disciplines.

12. See Robert S. Elwood, Jr., *Alternative Altars* (Chicago: Univ. of Chicago Press, 1979), 29.

13. See Robert Cohn, *The Shape of Sacred Space* (Chico, Calif.: Scholars Press, 1981).

14. See Victor Turner and Edith Turner, *Image and Pilgrimage in Christian Culture* (New York: Columbia Univ. Press, 1978).

15. An illustration of the value of the term "communitas": Shortly after I retired, I received a mimeographed letter from a friend in the campus ministry asking for suggestions concerning a "faith and life" community being formed by students and faculty in the university. I had a strong distaste for "faith and life" experiments in the university in the sixties; I thought they were "too pious" and shut off from the university, and so I threw the letter away. Then I thought, "Gee! Here you have spent twenty-five years at University Lutheran Church and have seen hundreds of persons coming through, worshiping, studying, and serving under you, and you can't even talk of a community." Someone has said that working as a campus pastor in a changing university is like a hen's trying to lay an egg on an escalator! All those you have invested yourself in leave just when they would be ready to settle down to a community. But then I thought of the word "communitas," a word referring to a temporary fellowship that has caught a common vision. I thought of the thousands of graduates with whom I keep in contact, and the shared experience that charges their vision. And I wrote back suggesting that we already had a communitas. Of course my friend was not pleased. But I think that someone should give due credit to this sort of fellowship on the way, a sort of liminal association.

16. See Mary Douglas, *Natural Symbols* (New York: Pantheon Books, 1973).

17. See Daniel F. Polish and Eugene J. Fisher, eds., *Liturgical Foundations of Social Policy in the Catholic and Jewish Traditions* (Notre Dame, Ind.: Univ. of Notre Dame Press, 1983).

MODEL FIVE:
LEADERSHIP IN THE CIVIC SPACE

1. In New England, one encounters the expectation that the ordained minister will be the moral voice of the community. The Jewish rabbi has as teacher traditionally had an analogous function. Roman Catholic priests are supposed to tell their people what to do in every situation. My fellow campus ministers in the sixties felt that they should exhibit a clear example of action in the civil-rights struggle.

2. I grew up in Ithaca, New York (pop. 17,004), and was active in civic affairs as a growing boy; I was president of Marion College, Marion, Virginia (pop., about 5,000); most of my ministry was in Cambridge, Massachusetts (pop., about 98,000).

3. In this paragraph, I hint at the situation with Lutherans from continental Europe; certainly the civic space was a new concept to them. Later I refer to Roman Catholics.

4. I often wonder why we find so many Roman Catholic laity going into politics or public-sphere occupations. Once there they serve as bridges for their people.

5. The church was Immanuel Lutheran Church, Cottman Avenue and Palmetto Street, in Philadelphia—in the outlying part of the city known as the Northeast.

6. This was in Marion, Virginia.

7. This was in Augusta, Georgia.

8. This was to Cambridge, Massachusetts.

9. The Ministerial Association had difficulty in getting the ministers from Central Square to keep coming to a group dominated by Harvard Square. A few black ministers came, but they soon separated into their own group, as black consciousness began to rise. Our study involved twenty religious communities—about half the non-Catholic churches. The Roman Catholics started to take an interest in the midsixties, as a result of Vatican II.

10. These agencies were established as advocacy organizations. They were protected in order to give voice and control to the underprivileged. The aim was certainly noble; the performance was difficult. The staff we hired always made alliances with the representatives of the underprivileged. The dynamics, however, were extremely hostile to efficient work. Pressure to withdraw was put on citizens representing the whole and those representing the helping institutions. They did withdraw and left the program in confusion.

11. This was at the World Conference on Faith and Science, at M.I.T. in the summer of 1978.

12. From my unpublished paper "The Associational Life of Cambridge: A Case Study," ca. 1976.

13. See Michael Balfour and Julian Frisby, *Herman von Moltke: A Leader against Hitler* (London: Macmillan & Co., 1972).

14. See John Curtis Raines, *Attack on Privacy* (Valley Forge, Pa.: Judson Press, 1974).